HIDDEN
MANNA
(Revised)

By

Rayola Kelley

Hidden **M**anna **P**ublications

HIDDEN MANNA (Revised)

Original *HIDDEN MANNA* Copyrighted © 1994 by Rayola Kelley and Jeannette Haley. **Revised edition** copyright © 2006 & 2023 by Rayola Kelley

ISBN: 978-1-7347503-3-1

Cover Paintings of the four creatures: Jeannette Haley

Except where otherwise indicated, all Scripture quotations in this book are taken from the King James Version

Hidden Manna Publications
P.O. Box 3572
Oldtown, ID 83822
www.gentleshepherd.com

Facebook:
https://www.facebook.com/HiddenMannaPublications/

CONTENTS

Introduction 5

1. The Nature of Something 8
2. Introduction to the Natures 21
3. Submissive Nature 30
4. Stubborn Nature 40
5. Self-Assured Nature 50
6. Strong-Willed Nature 58
7. Reality Vs. Perception 66
8. Counterfeit Repentance 76
9. The Process 85
10. Finding Our Place In Christ 95
11. The Reflection of Christ 112
12. Emitting the Fragrance of Christ 133
13. The Overcoming Church 147
14. A Final Thought 167

Bibliography 175
About the Author 176

INTRODUCTION

What does it mean to be human? Does humanity constitute a mystery too great to comprehend? Is it like much of creation— simple in function, but profound in possibilities? And, how does the essence of human nature affect us in our spiritual pilgrimage here on earth? It might serve us all well to consider these questions.

It appears as though many Christians are earnestly seeking the answers to these questions without any resolution. They look to man's philosophies, worldly relationships, and belief systems to come to terms with life in the hope of understanding themselves.

In spite of all of their searching, the breakdown of family, local churches, and society is escalating. As many people scramble to stop this destruction, lasting solutions are elusive.

For years, I have observed that people are in destructive cycles. Are these cycles a matter of habit or is there something behind their consistency? Cycles reveal that people respond a certain way to personal challenges and in their relationships with others. These predictable and clearly detectable responses can easily be observed in these individuals' reactions to reality and interaction with others.

Since cycles never deviate in attitude or action, there must be some kind of source or basis for the cycle other than habits. My conclusion was, if one could discover this base, the cycle could be stopped and consequences averted.

In 1986, the Lord, through various avenues, actually revealed to me the source behind the cycles found in people. This revelation was simple, but profound. I began to see how understanding the source of cycles would cut through the endless layers, facades, or cloaks people often hide behind to avoid accountability, repentance, and change.

As I began to confirm the information God had graciously revealed to me, a revelation of Jesus immerged. Obviously, God's heart was not to necessarily reveal the cycles of humanity, but to reveal Jesus in and through humanity. I was both awed and humbled by this reality.

The wickedness of the heart and the evil works of the flesh had hidden this revelation of Jesus that had been cleverly woven through the fiber of humanity. Even though this revelation can be seen in and confirmed by Scripture, it had been hidden from skeptical eyes and unbelieving hearts.

This unrevealed revelation brings us back to the formation of man in the Garden of Eden. Adam was created to reflect the glory of God. Sin marred the potential of man to serve as a reflection of God. Man eventually became a reflection of that which most influenced his selfish disposition and fleshly appetites.

When Jesus Christ died on the cross, it was God's way of restoring man to his original state of reflecting Him in the midst of a lost world. Sadly, many people fail to recognize what their position, purpose, and status is in light of God's eternal plan.

This book is to unveil the Hidden Manna of heaven. This material has the ability to call people back to the reality of God through the revelation of Jesus Christ. It will challenge readers to step outside of personal, destructive cycles to come higher in God, and to come to terms with their potential in the kingdom of heaven.

This information also gives viable solutions to help people become part of the answer instead of remaining part of the problem in destructive cycles. My prayer is that the reader will recognize his or her own particular cycle, step outside of it, turn around, call out to God, and begin to allow the very life and character of Jesus to be unveiled in his or her humanity for the glory of God.

1

THE NATURE OF SOMETHING

Do you realize everything has a nature? In my study of this word and its definitions, I concluded that it means, *"unchangeable characteristics that identify or define something"*. For example, God is not God in title or name. God is God because of who He is. His attributes constitute His nature as being deity, which identifies Him as God.

The Word of God is clear that there is only one God by nature, "Howbeit then, when ye knew not God, ye did service unto them which by <u>nature</u> are no gods" (Galatians 4:8). (Emphasis added.) The apostle Paul was clearly stating that before we knew the true God of heaven, we were paying homage to those who were not gods by nature.

God will not step outside of who He is. In other words, He will never cease to be God. He will always work in accordance with who He is. Most people think of God in light of what He can do, rather than who He is. They see Him as a storehouse, rather than a Person or entity whose power is disciplined by His unchangeable attributes. James 1:17 says, "Every good gift and every perfect gift is from above, and cometh down from the Father of lights, with whom is no variableness neither shadow of turning."

Hebrews 13:8 states, "Jesus Christ the same yesterday, and today, and forever."

Everything has a nature that identifies it. Every aspect of creation reacts according to its nature. An apple tree is an apple tree. It will never produce oranges regardless of similarities. A domestic cat may be part of a greater cat family that includes mountain lions, leopards, and tigers, but it will never be a mountain lion. The domestic cat is clearly distinguished from the rest of the species by certain characteristics, and it will never step outside of its nature or way of being.

Even though all animal and plant species fall into categories or families, they are clearly identified by their characteristics or nature. They stand distinct and unique in the midst of creation.

We know man stands unique in God's creation and heart. But, is there an order to man? Like the cat family, are there distinct categories among humanity? We know that man has been classified as homosapiens. Psalm 139:14 says this about man, "I will praise thee; for I am fearfully and wonderfully made: marvellous are thy works; and that my soul knoweth right well." As the different discoveries about our DNA are unveiled, one must conclude each person is fearfully and wonderfully made, as they personally stands distinct.

However, are there distinct natures found among people that clearly distinguish who they are and why they respond the way they do? Many people shrug off such a possibility. They believe themselves to be emotionally and intellectually complex, making them an exception to the rule. By being such an exception, they can hide behind aloofness, as they believe no one understands. Of course, this elitism all points to pride.

The arrogance of man chooses to believe that not only are people different, but that there is no explanation for their consistent cycles other than habits, family, friends, or religious influences. But, behind this façade is fear. People are a dichotomy. Many become isolated because they are not understood, while on the other hand they fear to be understood because there will be a level of accountability. They bounce back and forth between these two extremes like a ping-pong ball.

Is man beyond comprehension or does he have a nature that clearly identifies him? Certain people who have tried to understand the differences, yet similarities, of groups of people have come up with some amusing conclusions based on personality. These conclusions provide a weak, surface observation without merit or divine purpose. However, they have rightly concluded that there are four different groups found among people. Going a step further, my question was could this imply that there are four distinct natures (not mere "personalities") among humanity? The implications of this would be incredible. By understanding the basic makeup or the nature of a person, could destructive cycles and behavioral patterns be exposed and properly dealt with?

Surprisingly enough, four distinct natures have been identified among mankind. How do people's nature work in the scheme of their outward temperament and personality? On the next page is a good illustration on how nature fits into the way we each express ourselves.

Influence	Spirit	Motivation
Traits	Nature	Who I am
Heart	Disposition	Who I become
Environment	Prevailing Mood (Temperament)	Perception
Approach to life	Attitude	Manifestation
Fruits	Personality (Interaction/Reflection)	Who I allow myself to become

As you can see, the spirit motivating us will influence how the traits in our nature will express themselves through our disposition. Disposition sets up the prevailing mood or environment that will determine the direction of our perception. Will it be within or upward? Our perception will determine how we approach life. Our perception about life and God will be manifested in our attitude. Our attitude will determine the quality of our personality. Our countenance will ultimately reflect our true disposition. The disposition will influence what type of decisions we make in regard to life. Such decisions will determine who we ultimately allow ourselves to become as a person.

It is vital that we understand that the spirit and disposition will determine how the traits of our nature will be channeled, determining how our inner man will express itself. If the spirit is wrong, the disposition will be wrong. If the disposition is not regenerated, it will operate out of a wrong spirit.

It is a selfish disposition that was passed down from Adam to the rest of humanity. This fallen disposition is inclined towards sin and has the tendency to justify sin. It opposes God's rule in our lives, while tacking Him on in other ways. The only means to deal with this old, ungodly disposition is found in John 3:3 and 5. A person must be born again of Spirit and Water (the Word). Born again means a new disposition (a new heart and spirit) is being placed within an individual.[1] The new disposition is that of the very life of Jesus. It is inclined towards God and will prefer righteousness to personal darkness. Such a new disposition points to being a new creation. However, we must give way to the right spirit to ensure this disposition is brought forth in our lives. Sadly, many hold to their old disposition, while trying to disguise it behind a cloak of religion and good works. Therefore, the disposition reigning in us will determine the spirit motivating us, as well as how our traits will manifest themselves in our interaction with others.

Although uniquely set apart by appearance, personality, and talents, people respond and act according to their basic nature. Their nature not only identifies their cycle, but it also associates them to one of these four natures that can clearly be distinguished among humanity.

By understanding a person's particular nature, one can know how they perceive situations around them. A person will be able to cut through others' so-called "complexity" and "excuses" to address the real core issues of a problem.

By understanding people's basic nature, you will know their *need*. Every living thing has specific needs in order to live properly. Humans are not an exception to this rule. However,

---

[1] Ezekiel 36:26-27; 2 Corinthians 5:17; 1 Peter 1:23

peoples' needs go beyond physical existence to emotional and spiritual needs that produce well-being. A person's particular need in the area of emotional and spiritual well-being is their personal interpretation as to what constitutes love. A fulfilled need makes a person feel as if they belong. It gives a person a sense of purpose and fulfillment.

There are three such basic *needs* found among people. They are *emotional love*, *acceptance,* and *recognition*. Recognition splits off into two different categories. For example, there are people who need to be recognized for what they are trying to accomplish. And, then there are those who need to be recognized for who they are.

These needs push people into cycles with others. It sets up the environment around them. Environments can prove to be challenging, especially if there is conflict intruding into people's comfort zones. Ultimately, environments will determine the person's *desire*. There are three desires: *to be loved, have peace, or know joy or happiness.*

The emotional desire of a person reveals what is going on in their environment. For example, if a person desires love, they are revealing that their environment has a high percentage of hatred or unforgiveness. If the individual desires peace, they are declaring there is a lot of turmoil in their atmosphere. If the person says they desire joy or happiness, there is much despair in their environment.

The reason for unhealthy relationships and environments comes down to sin reigning in a situation. Because of Adam's rebellion, every person possesses a wrong disposition. Wrong disposition expresses itself in sin. This sin mars people's perception, abilities, and pursuits. For example, sin has perverted people's needs. This perversion causes conflict as people look to worldly relationships to get their needs met.

People clearly communicate love according to their own particular need. It is not unusual for them to be involved with others who have a different need. Therefore, as they communicate their perception of love to someone who has a different need, confusion, fear, and betrayal become byproducts. It is at this point that many conflicts arise in the relationship.

Conflicts or crises will cause people to respond according to their nature. This response begins in the attitude of self-sufficiency and responds in rebellion against God's authority. Rebellion points to independence. It is where a person "calls" the shots according to his or her terms. There are three main *attitudes* that point to self-sufficiency, and end in three rebellious corresponding actions. These attitudes set people up to act in the capacity of trying to be God in a matter. Such an attempt is a means of trying to control their reality or environment.

The first attitude is, *"I will deal with it, leave me alone."* This person *withdraws* into his or her mind to understand what is going on. Ultimately, reality is only changed in the mind, but it brings a false peace to the person as he or she becomes indifferent to what is happening around him or her. However, if understanding eludes the person, it throws him or her into confusion, fear, and depression.

The second attitude is, *"I can handle it, and I will prove it to you."* This individual struggles hard to handle all situations. People with this attitude try to control their environment or those in their environment, but most attempts end in defeat, producing frustration and anger. This person will avoid personal accountability by *justifying* unpleasant results at the expense of others or circumstances.

There are two forms of justification. There is the front door approach where the person is quick to up front justify away their actions with excuses. In fact, there is no end to this person's ability to fling out excuses. The second type of justification is where a person stands back, observes, and builds a case against the "culprit." In the right situation, this person will present their case and clear themselves of all accountability while declaring the other party guilty.

The final attitude is, *"I will take care of it, and I'll show you."* This is where the person considers what is going on, adjusts the situation to their ideas, and *makes it right* in their own sight. This type of person will either display shock or intolerance when there is opposition because they cannot see how they can be wrong.

These self-sufficient attitudes and rebellious actions mark the start of destructive cycles. These cycles point to independence where a person steps outside of God's perspective and takes matters into their own hands. At the heart of independence is *pride*. Pride that reigns, serves as an idol that torments and pushes a person. In fact, pride has four friends.

The first friend of pride is *fear*. Due to a fragile ego or an elevated perception of self, pride cannot afford to be wrong. Its fragile state causes it to operate in fear. Fear undermines power, love, and mental clarity.[2] There are four main fears that make people faint in their minds, hide from life, or run from reality. They are: *failure, rejection, incompetence,* and *losing control.*

Confusion is the next friend of pride. Pride does not deal in reality and when reality confronts it, the person will become confused. God is not a God of confusion, but of order.[3] Therefore, where confusion exists, one can find pride, the works of the flesh, or Satan.

Unbelief is another companion of pride. Since pride serves as an idol, it demands loyalty and obedience to its demands. As individuals put confidence in self, God resists them. Since God will be absent from much of the activity in their world, people begin to

---

[2] 2 Timothy 1:7
[3] 1 Corinthians 14:33

question His existence, commitment, or love, especially when consequences hit them. This doubt begins to undermine confidence in God, thereby, eroding away genuine faith. This will cause one to harden their heart towards God and walk in unbelief.

Delusion is the next prevalent friend of pride. It is opposite of truth. Truth is one of the greatest threats to pride. It will threaten, insult, and cause fear. It will reveal pride's wickedness and hypocrisy along with its many insecurities and insatiable appetites. There are three forms of pride found among people. They are: *conceit, selfishness,* and *pride* itself.

Conceit involves intellectual arrogance. It takes pride in what it knows and what it can do. It *focuses* on self while indirectly asking for attention. One of its clever ways to get attention is through fake nobility. Fake nobility states, "I know I am wretched, but aren't I humble about it." Even in depravity, this disguise of pride is exalted as being a helpless victim rather than a culprit. Once again, we are reminded that God resists pride and instructs and warns us to, "Be not wise in your own conceits" (Romans 12:16c).[4] When people encounter conceit, it often irritates them and causes the conceited person to lose credibility and appear foolish.

Selfishness is the next form of pride. It has to do with ego and vanity. This form of pride constantly *emphasizes* self. It wants your attention; therefore, it is always in competition and vying for top billing. For example, you may have had a bad day, but the person with selfishness will quickly rob you of the limelight by having a worse day or bringing up personal former successes in similar situations. This will cause tremendous frustration as you watch this selfishness either exalt itself or become a suffering martyr in every situation.

The third type of pride is what one would consider the epitome of arrogance, which is simply *pride* in all of its haughtiness. This

---

[4] James 4:6

type of pride operates within both the arenas of conceit and selfishness. For example, it operates from the conceits of the mind where it silently figures out how to be recognized, and then it plays the necessary game of selfishness to get its ego and vanity fed. Such pride demands your attention and becomes *preoccupied* with self. Ultimately, it must be in control of the situation. If pride is not properly recognized, it will regress into self-pity. Pride often intimidates people as it insists that others comply with its demands or the person will pay.

Pride is greatly entangled with a person's need. People think very highly of themselves.[5] Such high opinions often drive people in various attempts to get their need met. This drive is based on the lie that if real love is present, one is worthy of personal adoration or worship that comes through love, acceptance, or recognition. It is at this point where people get into games of control and manipulation with others.

These games cause conflict and destruction in relationships. There are three means people use to get their way: *words, attitudes, and actions.* In some cases, there can be a combination of these forms of control, but the results are the same— resentment, anger, and the breakdown of the relationship.

Obviously, people must step outside of these cycles. The problem is that most people don't recognize their own cycle. It is natural for them to operate according to their nature. In many cases, they believe they are right and feel they must hold the line. They fail to recognize that the bedrock of their disposition is the selfishness of pride. It causes unnecessary strife and ends in casualties.

Pride often deludes its victims as to personal problems. This delusion prevents the person from recognizing personal cycles. Out of mercy, God allows crisis and problems. These challenges

---

[5] Romans 12:3; Galatians 6:3

become a process. The process is geared towards the person's nature. The goal of this process is to bring the person to the end of their self-sufficiency and rebellion to face their need for God's intervention.

There are three different processes that individuals find themselves in. These processes are related to priceless gems: pearl, gold, or diamond. A *pearl* starts out as a grain of sand that finds its way into an oyster. This grain of sand begins to *irritate* the oyster, which in turn spits at the grain of sand. This simply means a pearl is hardened saliva, but it is desired and valued by many.

For people who go through a similar process, God will use a string of irritants that will cause them to snap under the pressure and seek one greater than self to understand the challenge. When they finally come to God, He can surround them with His perspective.

Other people go through a *gold* process. These people need to be separated from something. For some, they must go through a *sifting* process where they are separated from defeating factors in their lives. But, for others they must go through a *boiling* process where they must be separated from something that is intertwined with the very essence of self.

Diamonds begin as a piece of coal. Coal has some value, but is useless unless it is consumed by fire. However, a piece of coal has a greater potential, that of becoming a diamond. For coal to reach its greater potential, it must go through extreme heat and pressure. People who go through this process often find themselves facing extreme situations that could bring them to the abyss of destruction.

The Lord's heart is for His people to reach their potential in Him. This involves a process, and when His people come out on the other side, they will be priceless gems. One day, He will take these gems and place them in a crown that will reflect His glory.

The spiritual process is to *confront, challenge, and channel* the traits of each nature in order to change the person's disposition and behavior patterns. Even though people have a tendency to adopt the traits of those around them, the traits of their particular nature will be evident. These traits can be traced from a person's particular form of rebellion, not necessarily their personality. As you study the different traits of each nature, you will realize how they must be properly confronted in order to discern whether their traits must be disciplined or challenged. Once challenged, some traits must be mortified, allowing the rest of the traits to be channeled and brought under the control of God.

It is important to correctly discern the nature of a person to determine where they might be spiritually. For example, what would be considered normal for one person would be abnormal for another. There are three levels that people can operate within. They are: *balanced, unbalanced,* or *extreme.*

If a person is under God's authority, he or she will be balanced in his or her attitudes and responses. If a person is unbalanced, he or she is focused on self, which makes him or her self-centered and operating in a small world of rebellion, self-pity, and disillusionment. If a person is operating in extremes, then you can conclude Satan is on the scene.

This brings us to a very important point: *Who is ruling in your life?* Either God or Satan is the ruler. If Satan rules, it means sin is enslaving you and self is being exalted. If God reigns as your Savior and Lord, you can be assured of salvation and the work of sanctification.

Examine the following table and consider what your need, attitude, and response are. See if you can get a glimpse into your nature. Keep in mind most people never perceive themselves in the proper manner. This is why it can prove hard for some to see personal cycles and failures

SIMPLE PICTURE OF HUMANITY		
Deceptive Levels	I will *deal* with it, Leave me *alone*.	I will *handle* it, I will *prove* it.	I will *take care* of it, I will *show* you.
Rebellion Levels	*Withdraw* into mind.	*Justify* to avoid accountability.	*Make it right* in own sight.
Needs	Acceptance	Emotional Love	Recognition
Desires	Love	Peace	Joy/Happiness
Forms of Control and Manipulation	Words	Attitudes	Actions
Forms of Pride	Conceit (Focuses-Irritate)	Selfishness (Emphasize-Frustrate)	Pride (Preoccupy-Intimidate)
Types Found in Natures	Balanced (Under God)	Unbalanced (Self-centered)	Extreme (Demonic Influence)
Processes	Pearl (Irritants)	Gold (Friction/Boil)	Diamond (Heat/Pressure)
Three C's	Confront (Rebellion-Discipline)	Challenge (Mortify the Flesh)	Channel (Under the Spirit)

2
INTRODUCTION TO
THE NATURES

The nature information has been confused and compared with the four temperaments teaching and the worldly philosophy of psychology. It is neither. In the first chapter I made reference to the prevailing mood or temperament of a person. Temperaments determine the condition of one's environment. However, they can fluctuate according to situations, but people still react according to their nature.

The spirit and disposition will determine what a person becomes. This is why a person's disposition must be transformed and brought under the control of the Spirit of God to change any wrong prevailing temperament. Even though our temperament changes, we will continue to act according to our nature. The difference is that the Spirit is now regenerating our traits. People must recognize the tendencies and traits of their natures, and make sure they are properly confronted and channeled under the control of the Holy Spirit to reach their potential in Christ.

Psychology is the study of human behavior, and generally excuses away personal sin and accountability. As you study its origins, you can conclude that it falls into the category of the worthless philosophies of men, the world, and spirit guides. The Apostle Paul made this statement in Colossians 2:8, "Beware lest any man spoil you through philosophy and vain deceit, after the tradition of men, after the rudiments of the world, and not after Christ."

The questionable origins and spirit of psychology has made the use of it in the Church a heated debate in Christendom. The Word is clear that God is the true counselor, and that people can only be set free by His truth. Truth means a person realistically comes to terms with his or her disposition in order to overcome and reach their personal potential in Christ. The nature information simply explains the behavioral patterns of the four different natures in light of how the selfish disposition of pride works within the person.

Is the nature information legitimate? One must test the spirit behind it to see if it lines up to the Spirit of God and the truth of the Word of God. I have been working with this information since it was revealed to me in 1986. Women from my Bible Study tested it out. They would take the information home and try it out on their families. The results often shocked them as they began to see through the maze of cloaks that even their own family members hid behind. As they cut through the games of rebellion and control, distinct consistent patterns immerged. Amazingly, even in its infant stages, four distinct natures could clearly be identified.

Over the next four years the information expanded. It was discovered that individuals are not as complex as they often appear to be. By understanding the nature of a person, one could cut through the excuses and games to address, properly confront, minister, or call a person to accountability. Each time the information was tried or presented there was an expectancy that it would break down at any moment. However, each time it was confirmed.

The nature information even transcended gender, culture, and race. The information was presented to Koreans who still adhered to their culture. I expected to find inconsistency in the information due to cultural influences. Once again it was confirmed. The

Koreans clearly identified their particular nature along with those of their friends. One Korean lady testified how she had felt isolated in America, but after attending the seminar she realized there were Americans with the same nature as her. She no longer felt alone or isolated.

Another interesting test had to do with gender. There is a well-preserved assumption or myth that women are more emotional than men. I personally questioned this logic because as a woman, my emotions come out last in my cycle, while I have met men who were clearly emotional. These men's emotions often manifested in frustration and anger. As a result, I witnessed confusion among the sexes, while occasionally questioning my own normalcy. Later I discovered that culture often defines people based on their gender rather than their person, character, and abilities. This has caused a tremendous amount of personal conflict, as well as identity crises.

In the unveiling of these natures, it was discovered that emotions surface at different stages for the different natures. For example, there is one nature that is emotional up front. Whether the individual is male or female, he or she feels very deeply about things, and displays emotional fervor in causes and beliefs.

On the other end of the spectrum, another nature goes through a process of mental evaluation until feelings are encountered. For people of this nature, it can actually take as much as a couple of weeks (or in some cases, years) for their emotions to catch up to them. In one incident, it took two weeks for a woman's sorrow over her grandfather's death to catch up with her. At the funeral she thought herself to be unfeeling. Two weeks later a minor incident caused her to fall apart. It was at this point that her grandfather's death had emotionally penetrated her.

In one of the Hidden Manna Seminars, I encountered a skeptic who questioned the information. He had come because of the insistence of his wife and friends. As I began to share the

23

information, he started to relax. This man was the emotional type. In the past, he could not understand his enthusiasm, sensitivity, and his emotional fervor or outbursts. He had questioned his normalcy as a man. In the seminar he discovered that he was quite normal for his nature. In fact, God had used his emotional fervor to make him a bold witness. This brought tremendous peace to his soul, and even his daughter noticed that he possessed an inner peace that had not been there in the past.

The next weekend after the seminar, this man and his wife celebrated their wedding anniversary. Their time together was rewarding and precious because of the special insight they received about their individual natures. The following Tuesday, the man had a heart attack and went home to be with the Lord. His wife was thankful for the impact the nature information had brought to his life and their relationship in the short time they had remaining together.

On another occasion, an educator was ready to put her 13-year-old daughter into a detention center. She asked me to meet with her after she overheard me talk about the nature information. As she described her daughter, her nature was quickly identified. The mother was then advised how to properly confront her daughter according to the young girl's nature. The mother was also told that she would be pleasantly surprised to see that her daughter would probably display integrity. A couple of months later I touched base with the mother. She shared that her daughter was responding in a constructive way, and she was pleasantly surprised to discover that she had good character.

In one of my first seminars in Washington State, a woman recognized the nature of her daughter who had tried to commit suicide a few weeks earlier. She immediately applied the information, not only in regards to her daughter, but her whole family. She immediately witnessed results.

In another situation a young girl was acting contrary to her nature. In questioning her mother, she admitted that she and her husband suspected that the little girl had been molested. I realized that what she was displaying was shame. We ministered to her and dealt with her shame. The last time I saw her, the shame was gone and she was acting in accordance to her nature.

This information fascinates people and often appeases the intellect. Like the Word of God, when this information is kept on an intellectual plane and not put into practice, it becomes useless. Spiritual truths of God are meant to change attitudes and relationships. This is true for this information. When put into proper practice it has proven to stop destructive cycles, change the disposition of a person, and has been priceless in marriage relationships and for parents dealing with their children.

As previously stated, there are four distinct natures that are veiled in humanity. These four natures are:

Submissive

Stubborn

Self-Assured

Strong-Willed

Clear pictures or impressions come into people's minds when they hear or read the names of these natures. One individual asked me how I came up with them. She considered a couple of the names to be offensive.

I went to the Lord and asked Him the reason for the names. He revealed to me the names were based on the wall of protection. People put this wall up when they feel that someone does not understand them. Without proper understanding, a person does not feel that they can afford to be vulnerable because the individual in question cannot be trusted. Therefore, the person will put up a wall that will protect them from being hurt. For example, *submissive* people are not wimps, but they can quickly put up a wall of fear and submit to it.

The *stubborn* person is not always obstinate, but when threatened, they will put up an obstinate wall. In this state a stubborn person will not only refuse to move, but will dare anyone to try to knock down the wall.

The *self-assured* nature does not mean the person is sure of self. In fact, this type of individual can be very unsure of self and erect two different walls to protect or hide insecurities and uncertainties to maintain an outward facade. One wall can be emotional while the other one immovable and harsh.

The wall of the *strong-willed* person is actually comprised of all of their traits. This person can be dynamic, and will have a sense of infallibility. This individual's wall can be intimidating and immovable to those who encounter his or her wall.

By understanding a person's nature, you can know how to keep the person's wall down. This allows for communication and keeps open the avenue that will help to confront isolation, vain imaginations, moral deviation, and depression.

Each nature has different needs, forms of pride, and different means of manipulation and control. They process information differently, confront challenges according to their areas of strengths, and approach life from a different perspective. As a result, there are a lot of speculations and assumptions going on in people who have a different nature. People marry individuals with different natures. This often makes a spouse feel as if he or she has married someone from another planet.

The diversities in these four natures cause pride to raise its ugly head. This is where the judgmental "board" blinds a person to their own personal faults as they focus in on what are considered the other person's offenses.[1] These misunderstandings or evaluations cause people to walk in judgmentalism or condemnation towards those they harshly judge. Both of these attitudes cause problems in relationships as they express themselves in fear, anger, or arrogance.

When people recognize natures, it not only allows them to confront or approach others effectivity, but it helps them to accept who they are. Some people compare themselves to others because they have a hard time accepting the way God made them.[2] As a result, they find themselves in an identity crisis as they struggle to find their place in the kingdom of God and recognize their form of leadership. The Apostle Paul said this about such comparison, "For we dare not make ourselves of the number, or compare ourselves with some that commend themselves: but they measuring themselves by themselves, and comparing themselves among themselves, are not wise" (2 Corinthians 10:12).

It is only as people accept the way God made them that they can accept God for who He is. Because many people cannot accept themselves, they unknowingly question God's reasoning. In their mind they represent a flaw in God's plan, rather than the potential to express Jesus Christ in a unique way.[3]

The beautiful discovery is that Christ is veiled or hidden in humanity. Once the Manna of heaven is unveiled in a person, they will discover the beauty of life, and will be able to impart this Manna to others.[4]

The question is, are you ready to discover in what way Jesus can be expressed in your humanity? Are you ready to take the journey through your inner person to see how you respond? Are

---

[1] Matthew 7:1-5
[2] Psalm 139:14-24
[3] Romans 8:29; 2 Corinthians 3:18
[4] John 6:32-40; Revelation 2:17

you open enough to discover the makeup of your cycle so you can step outside of it and become a solution rather than part of the problem?

As you begin this journey of personal discovery, there are a few facts you need to remember.

You have only <u>one</u> nature. Many people become confused because they display traits of other natures. People of other natures do influence us, and we tend to adopt some of their traits. I call these <u>secondary</u> <u>traits</u>. You must discover your own basic nature, and then you can properly begin to distinguish the traits of your particular nature. This means you must come to terms with your form of rebellion and need. It is hard for people to recognize their rebellion because it is so natural for them to respond the way they do. In fact, it seems logical, practical, and justifiable, but rebellion comes down to dealing with, handling, or taking care of a matter in one's personal strength. Personal strength points to pride, self-sufficiency, and independence.

When people first learn this information, they do not like what they see about their nature. Some become very upset and depressed. It proves what the Bible has long advocated, that there is no good thing in man's flesh.[5] The purpose of this information is to recognize the different aspects of our nature so we can reach our potential in Christ. The explanation of each nature is based strictly on how the particular nature operates when it is in its unregenerate state.

If you are a mature Christian, it might be hard to recognize yourself. Self-denial, the application of the cross, and the sanctifying work of the Spirit can change much in your disposition, but the nature is still in place, but now it will be transformed to reflect Jesus, rather than the old man.

---

[5] Romans 3:10; 7:18

Keep in mind; we are the ones who least know ourselves. People have an unrealistic idea of who they think they are. Sometimes it is hard to recognize one's own nature, but those who live with us know us quite well. If you are in confusion about your nature, ask those around you how you really act and respond in situations.

With these points in mind, it is time to begin this incredible journey to discover how God made you, and what He wants to accomplish in you. Your life will never be the same, your relationships will change, and your perception of God will be enlarged to embrace the revelation and unveiling of Christ in your life.

3

SUBMISSIVE NATURE

People with a submissive nature often come across as *sweet* and *quiet*. They are considered the most compliant child or one of the nicest of individuals. This outward sweetness usually hides a great deal of fear. In fact, the walls of protection that people erect hide some form of fear, but for submissive people, their actual rebellious wall is *fear*. This wall is quickly erected in situations that the submissive person does not understand or may have to *confront*.

Due to the sweet exterior and the inward fear, submissive people can send confusing messages to others. Confusion causes problems in their relationships because these people need to be *accepted*, but often feel they are accepted only if they are compliant. This makes them feel as if they must earn acceptance by being good, which may produce resentment, anger, and rebellion in them.

A submissive person seeks to understand the mechanics of something. They have a mind like a computer. It is full of compartments that contain various "file cabinets." Within these "cabinets" are options that can be explored or considered in the right situation. Because of how they process information, they are very *persevering* in their attempts to find the best solution to their problem or challenge in order to avoid any unpleasant confrontation.

Submissive people have great confidence in their ability to figure something out. Their attitude is, *"Leave me alone, I will deal* with it." When faced with a challenge, they *withdraw* into their mind and begin to *analyze* possible options. James 4:8 states, "Draw nigh to God, and he will draw nigh to you." This person is actually drawing away from God instead of closer to Him. However, the submissive people's great confidence in their ability to reason something out blinds them to the reality that they are in competition or opposition against God's wisdom.

Submissive people are very *methodical* in their approach to a problem. Their speed of processing information also determines the speed with which they do all of their activities. They will only move as fast as their mind is able to process information. I have seen people of this nature with different speeds. Some move fast, others have a medium speed, and others are slow. They usually have one consistent pace. In fact, if this person is pushed to move beyond their speed, they can become overwhelmed. This is when you might find this type of individual parked behind a wall of fear. Each time you try to push the submissive person to move or go faster, the wall of fear can often be reinforced.

These individuals will seek out the best option, method, program, or diplomatic way to deal with a problem. Sadly, submissive people do not realize that exaltation of their mind is idolatry. An unregenerate mind is at enmity with God.[1] It is unable to discern the things of God, causing a person to walk in the flesh rather than in the Spirit.

The *mind* is where the submissive person's rebellious cycle begins. It leads the person down a path of *dramatization* and depression as they lose *perspective*. These people actually begin to develop ruts in their mind. As different challenges confront them, they stick every challenge, bit of information, or conclusion in a compartment to consider or deal with it later. Amazingly, these

---

[1] Romans 8:5-8

people can even have a compartment for the things they choose to ignore.

Eventually, all of the compartments become full. When this happens, submissive people cease to be compliant and even-tempered, and become *obnoxious*. Attitudes begin to stick out as they become *unmanageable* in their responses, intense as they hide further behind their wall of fear, and unbearable to live with. By this time, they are out of control and out of perspective. For this type of individual, it is like falling off an emotional cliff into a pit; and, climbing out of it will take everything in them to come once again into emotional balance. This is why Proverbs 3:5 serves as a valuable instruction to these people, "Trust in the LORD with all thine heart; and lean not unto thine own understanding."

Emotions are the last reaction that comes out of this person. When this type of person begins to show emotions, you know that situations are catching up to them, and will eventually overwhelm them. In fact, these people's mental compartments usually fill up with unresolved issues that have been put on the shelf until another day. At this stage of the cycle, understanding is clearly eluding the submissive person, making them feel that their life is out of control. It is from this premise that these individuals have a tendency of withdrawing even deeper into their mind.

As already alluded to the biggest problem with submissive people is that all of this mental exercise comes down to them *avoiding outright confrontation* with someone, or simply facing the reality of an environment that is becoming confusing as it increasingly spins out of control. This avoidance is very self-centered and self-serving, but it is often considered noble by the submissive person.

Submissive people refuse to see that their unwillingness to face problems up front has nothing to do with protecting or watching out for the other person, but with protecting self of possible conflict or consequences that might inevitably make them appear as a *failure*. Such avoidance is a form of control and manipulation that refuses to face the selfishness behind the game that is being played. This *fake nobility* that is displayed often covers up the submissive people's greatest initial fear—that of failure. Their unwillingness to confront problems because of their fear of failure throws them into cycles in their relationships with others including God.

This cycle begins with the submissive person trying to avoid, comply, or please someone to keep the peace as a means to avoid conflict. Such a response requires a submissive person to play the game to avoid confrontation. The natural tendency for people in a relationship with a submissive person, who has avoided properly confronting them for wrong attitudes or actions, is to take advantage of their reluctance to challenge the situation. When the submissive person plays these people's game, it usually unleashes the monster of pride and selfishness in them rather than subduing it. Due to pride, these individuals become more demanding, abusive and disrespectful towards the submissive individual. The submissive person struggles with how to properly deal with the other person or issue as the matter escalates, while striving to maintain their sweetness and nobility. As the submissive struggles, they devise well-planned statements that are meant to stop the other person in their tracks by putting them in their place, thereby, avoiding confrontation.

Submissive people are good at using *words* as a means to control and manipulate. In some cases, it works, while in other situations, it simply prolongs a matter. In the end, submissive people are left with a lot of *unresolved issues* that will develop into a tidal wave that will eventually threaten to destroy their mental and emotional well-being and their relationships.

Unresolved issues will eventually bury these individuals. This is where the submissive person will give up and spiral downward into depression. These individuals can retreat behind barricades of eating disorders, alcoholism, drug abuse, and imaginary or exaggerated physical problems. These excessive behaviors have three possible sources behind them: 1) They serve as forms of control; 2) they are a means of getting attention; and 3) they become ways of self-destruction.

Extreme behaviors in submissive people that are not properly challenged can cause the submissive person to toy with the option of *suicide*. When a submissive person is at this point, they are in major depression. It is a sign that the person is out of perspective and needs to be properly confronted. Sadly, this person rarely shares what they are thinking about. Suicide, therefore, is often this person's dangerous little secret.

Pride in Action

A submissive person's form of pride is hard to detect. In fact, their pride would be considered a covert pride. Because these people's pride is not obvious, they actually view themselves as superior to others whose pride may be more obvious.

Submissive people's arrogance can clearly be observed in relationships. I knew of a submissive woman who displayed steady calmness in most situations. Her husband, who was more expressive about his feelings, would especially vent in traffic. She viewed his actions as unacceptable and felt superior to him. This woman was blinded to her form of pride, a sin that God resists. In fact, it is the covert sins that will sink a person more than outward disobedience.

The pride that motivates a submissive person is *conceit*. Although conceit has a certain air about it and causes *irritations* in others, it is hard to detect in this type of individual because it is not expressed in obtrusive self-exaltation. In fact, this individual is often considered to have a low or no self-esteem, and will nobly throw the attention elsewhere to avoid being noticed. The reason is that the submissive person wants to be left alone in their world. If submissive people do emerge from their self-made mental world, they will want you to know how smart, humble, sweet, wise, or good they are. Conceit ultimately translates into intellectual pride. It takes pride in what it knows and can do.

These people perceive themselves to be *wise* in all their ways. They will try to reason with others about their way of doing things. If they encounter someone who will not agree or tolerate their reasoning or condescending air, they will nobly give way to the other person and become a suffering martyr. This fake nobility still leaves them on top of the game because it exhibits more honor than the one who refuses to receive wise instruction.

Even though submissive people outwardly give way to someone else's perception, they never give in mentally. They usually maintain their way of thinking, and will go back to the drawing board to devise a cleverer argument for the next encounter. If the issue is not resolved according to their way of thinking, they will end up overanalyzing, which causes them to appear unreasonable, foolish, or obsessive. In fact, people who are trying to deal with a submissive person at this state would refer to them as being *pigheaded.*

Conceit's greatest disguise is *false humility.* False humility is nothing more than worldly remorse.[2] Worldly remorse will take some accountability for failure, but it is to make such individuals feel they have properly conceded on a matter. Since they have come to terms with it in their mind, they figure that you need to get off their back and leave them alone.

The reason most submissive people fall short of true repentance is because they simply work it out in their mind. They perceive that now that they have worked it out in their mind, it is reality. These people have failed to realize that they have not

---

[2] 2 Corinthians 7:10

changed their mind. They have simply added another conclusion to one of their compartments. Since they have not changed their mind, their heart maintains the same inclinations that keep them on the same path or course. In other words, nothing has changed.

Changed lives are the fruit of true repentance. When those around submissive people do not see the change, they will not give them the desired acknowledgment. After all, submissive people work hard to bring everything together in their mind. To not be recognized for such a feat is considered unfair. This is when fake nobility turns into self-pity. These people began to feel sorry for themselves because they have done everything to play the game and cannot understand why others will not recognize their attempts. Once again, these individuals come out on top in their minds as they become victims.

Like all pride, unchallenged conceit will eventually lead its devoted followers into delusion. This delusion creates a sick little world of depression, obsession, and utter ridiculousness. Ultimately, the submissive person becomes a fool in their own conceits.

Overcoming

Submissive people must come to terms with their traits in order to overcome. They must be surrounded by God's perspective much like the grain of sand is when being formed as a *pearl*. One of the traits they must honestly *confront* is their sweetness. This trait is not part of the fruit of the Spirit. Rather, it is part of their selfish disposition. This sweetness gives a false sense of "goodness" to these people. They hide behind it to avoid confrontation. Their unwillingness to confront falls in with the sins of omission, where righteousness is being omitted in a matter. This unwillingness is also a subtle form of unbelief because it shows that those who avoid confronting life do so out of fear and complacency.

Submissive people must realize that their sweetness often serves as a cloak to cover up their true depravity.[3] It is not an expression of Jesus, but a means to receive desired acceptance and undeserved recognition. Therefore, this trait must give way to the sanctifying work of the Holy Spirit.

Certain traits must be disciplined. For the submissive person, they must discipline their analytical mind. Overanalyzing causes this person to *dramatize.* In order to keep their minds balanced, submissive people must withdraw into God. This allows their earthly wisdom to give way to the true wisdom of heaven.[4] Godly wisdom means one will have God's perspective. And, it is His perspective that ensures balance in a submissive person's life.

There are other traits that must be *mortified* or put to death. The submissive traits that fall into this category are fear and conceit. Fear demands worship from its subject. As long as submissive people give in to it, they will be hindered from reaching their potential in Christ. When submissive people encounter fear, they must step back from the wall, decide to step through it, ask Jesus to take their hand, and leave fear behind as they take steps of faith through fear's darkness.

Submissive people must realize that their conceit is perverted and earthly wisdom. Once they agree with God's evaluation about it, they must ask Him to reveal how it works in their life and to give them a hatred for it. Pride can only be overcome by a repulsive hatred towards it. Submissive people must realize that conceit does not make them wise, but sets them up to play the fool.

There are traits that must be *channeled.* Submissive people must learn to withdraw into God. This means they will be putting their confidence in Him, rather than in their minds. This allows the Holy Spirit to properly channel all information, in order to bring

---

[3] Galatians 5:22-23; James 4:17; John 15:22
[4] James 3:13-17

37

forth God's perspective. Once the mind is transformed, the submissive person will gain an understanding of God's way. It is this understanding that establishes the submissive person on the immovable Rock of Ages and brings peace to their mind.[5]

Confrontation

How do you properly confront a submissive person? You must first recognize when they are in their cycle. There are two indicators that this type of person is in a destructive cycle. The initial sign are bad attitudes. Submissive people do not have strong attitudes per se. Therefore, any sign of an attitude means that they are overwhelmed and their compartments are full.

The second indicator is unbalanced or extreme behavioral patterns. For example, if a submissive person is overly emotional or obnoxious, there is something amiss in their world. Obviously, there are unresolved issues that are filling up their compartments.

If the submissive person is very withdrawn, this is a big warning signal. You must not allow them to remain in their world unchallenged. Such extreme behavior points to depression, which can include suicidal thoughts and plans. These people will be tight-lipped about such plans unless asked. However, if you show *acceptance* and firmly challenge their perception with the facts, they will simply do their submissive thing by automatically withdrawing and considering what you have presented.

As you consider how you confront different people, you will begin to see how you actually use a person's nature against them in confrontation. You do this by using the person's need and way of processing information to get their attention. Once you have people's attention, you can effectively speak into their lives. For example, you show a submissive person acceptance to keep their

---

[5] Isaiah 26:3

wall down. By understanding that such an individual analyzes all information, you must be ready to firmly give these people the facts. These facts will challenge the submissive person's perspective. Granted, these people will try to occasionally deter you by being obnoxious or running you around with reason. Do not be sidetracked by either detour. Once the submissive person gains perspective, they are most likely to admit when they have been out of line since they will avoid all possible confrontation.

When giving this nature the facts, avoid being harsh or placating. If you are harsh with this type of individual, you will encounter his or her wall of fear. If you try placating the submissive person, they will perceive it as a game and will lose respect for you.

4

STUBBORN NATURE

The greatest struggle for the stubborn-natured person is with their *emotions*. Unlike submissive people whose emotions come out at the last part of his or her cycle, emotions are the first thing you encounter with the stubborn individual. In fact, these people wear their emotions on their sleeves.

The emotional level of a stubborn person makes them *personable*. Often this front hides insecurities and doubts while keeping others at a distance. It is also a means for some stubborn people to con others. This is a form of control and manipulation that will eventually be exposed for the game it is, causing them to lose credibility.

The emotions of stubborn people run deep, and will cause confusion and conflict in their worlds. These emotions have almost a tormenting force behind them that often causes these people to seek after relief, pleasure, and satisfaction through various avenues. They can become *impulsive* about filling up their worlds with things or activities that make them feel good, or will satisfy their need to bring meaning and purpose to their often-chaotic world.

These means are always temporary, which can send them on unusual or sporadic searches. Needless to say, trying to bring undisciplined emotions under control can prove to be very overwhelming to these people. As a result, they often live in a dream world while unsuccessfully trying to manipulate and adjust their world to their particular fantasies. If stubborn people run out of fantasies or the means to satisfy their emotions due to harsh reality that remains constant, they will close down their emotions. This will create a zombie who will be expressionless due to utter hopelessness.

Stubborn people need to feel *love*. This love is an emotional love where others actually enter into the emotional world with them. For the other three natures who do not understand the emotional plight of these people, it can be both frustrating and traumatic. They do not know how to calm the emotional beast that often rises up within stubborn people. This beast can become explosive and abrasive.

This type of individual feels the need to earn this emotional love. There are four reasons for this outlook: 1) Stubborn people feel vulnerable in the area of love because of being gullible; 2) they strive to be indispensable to others to avoid experiencing rejection; 3) they have high standards that demand reformation; and 4) they need proof of love; therefore, they conclude they must earn love. The gullibility of a stubborn person comes down to their need to be transparent with others. This is to ensure that people will simply love them for who they are.

Stubborn people try to become indispensable to those they love and care about because of their own insecurities and fears. Their greatest fear is *rejection*. They do everything to avoid this feeling, only to find rejection haunting them as they are *misunderstood* and often taken for granted.

People of this nature have very high *standards*. These standards not only put unrealistic pressure on them along with those in their environment, but they actually box them in. Such standards are meant to bring discipline to the stubborn person's emotions and environment, but instead of bringing order to the environment, these standards often cause these people to become hard and unmerciful. These high standards make them very judgmental and skeptical about anything that does not initially line up with their unrealistic values or undisciplined emotions.

The stubborn person requires proof of love. Sadly, this proof may be insatiable and unrealistic. These people can put up a fuss or fight, and expect those who care about them to fight for them, not with them. Even though they want others to fight for them, they either put up resistance to such attempts, or they emotionally run people around. Those who are dealing with this type of nature find themselves fighting with these individuals. This causes those who are trying to contend with them to throw up their hands in utter hopelessness or walk away in frustration.

The emotional stubborn person feels deeply about personal beliefs. These people can be *persistent* in their pursuits. This happens when they get caught up with causes that will rob them of valuable time, take them on detours, or lead to obsessions. It is not unusual for these people to get caught up with the causes of the underdog because they have a deep sense of loyalty, as well as hate unfairness. In the process, such causes can turn into obsessions that often throw common sense and reality out the door. These obsessions imply total indifference and delusion about reality.

Stubborn people can display common sense. Their *practical* approach to life, decisions, and situations can cause those with a different nature to experience frustration and anger. In most cases, a balanced and realistic stubborn person does see the end result of situations, but due to his or her emotional level, others rarely take this individual seriously. Problems, therefore, are not averted and the stubborn person is proven to once again be correct. This can cause resentment and jealousy with those who did not understand or respect the practical, simple side of this type of individual.

The stubborn individual strives hard to maintain or control their environment to keep on top of their emotions. This need to control the environment to keep emotions intact is often considered controlling and manipulative by others. Such a perspective will cause more *friction* for the stubborn person who has failed to realize they must bring their personal emotions under control before their world can have order.

Stubborn people are consistent in their emotional patterns. The emotional cycle usually starts when *plans* are *interrupted*. These people try hard to organize their day so they can complete the many demands or responsibilities of their world. For example, a stubborn person may have 20 different activities on their list. These people actually can make plans in their mind right down to the last minute as to what they are going to do. Then, someone adds one more demand; the *pressure* begins to build because this individual no longer feels emotionally on top of it. This becomes obvious as they begin to *complain* about all of their responsibilities. This is followed by *strong attitudes*.

If the emotional momentum is not properly dealt with, *explosive anger* follows. This anger breeds insult, offense, hurt, and anger in others. The results leave the stubborn person experiencing doubts, insecurities, and *guilt*. Satan starts to support this case of guilt, opening the door of condemnation. *Condemnation* will send this person into hopelessness or *depression*.

Stubborn people feel the depths of depression. They often fear it, and will do everything to avoid this unbearable pit. They actually run from it through activities, relationships, and substance abuse.

Due to the fickleness of their emotions, stubborn people are often *misunderstood*, causing them personal hurts and wounds. These people perceive themselves as *handling* any situation, and given enough time will *prove* it to others. Eventually, reality will collide with their world in the form of interrupted plans or rejection. They stand in confusion as they consider everything they did to get the necessary *approval* from those around them. After all, they have been giving, complimentary, and gone out of their way to become indispensable. When stubborn people do not receive the necessary acknowledgement or reaction from others, they can feel rejected, used, and abused. These feelings will produce hurt that turns into anger and *complaints*. These complaints can cause others around the stubborn person to scramble in an attempt to change a stubborn person's environment to keep the monster of selfishness at bay. To handle these emotions, a stubborn person will stuff them. Unresolved issues will create frustration, moodiness, and attitudes in them.

Once the stubborn person has stuffed an unresolved issue, they become a time bomb as the emotional momentum begins to build up like a volcano. It is a matter of time before something will cause them to explode, leaving others in a state of confusion and chaos.

This is when stubborn people come to the harsh reality that they cannot handle it. They begin to *justify* their reactions at the expense of their environment. For example, if it was not for so or so, or this or that, they would have never exploded. Quickly, they release themselves from personal responsibilities while trying to handle the guilt they feel under the barrage of excuses.

These excuses allow them to erect a *stubborn* wall of protection. This wall declares that no one will pass beyond it. It implies the stubborn person must maintain their justification about a matter and will not sway from their stand. At this point stubborn people are viewed as being *bullheaded*. Not only do they refuse to be moved, but if challenged, they will charge and push back all opposition. But, in spite of the justification and wall, the guilt remains intact.

Stubborn people desire to be stopped at the point of justification in order to silence their guilt. Although they can act unreasonably when confronted, the stubborn person does not know how to stop themselves after a certain emotional point or silence the onslaught of personal excuses. In my experience with these individuals, I have found that their excuses are a means of trying to convince themselves that they are not guilty. If they do not come to truth about their personal involvement in a situation, they can become deluded. This means they create ruts in their mind where excuses become a truth rather than a point of self-justification and self-delusion. When stubborn people are in this type of rut, their bullheadedness becomes apparent as the truth is pushed aside, and they become defensive, unreasonable, angry, and in some cases bullies.

Due to their *undisciplined emotions*, these people desire proper discipline, but will rebel against any form of control and manipulation. Although these people can come across as pushy, they will not tolerate being pushed or controlled by others. Sadly, those who are around them try to control or manipulate them because they are afraid of how they might react in different environments or situations. To stubborn people, such attempts are like putting a red flag in front of a charging bull. Needless to say, they will oblige and charge.

When Pride Hits the Scene

Pride is the last trait that enters the scene in the stubborn person's cycle, but when it does, it leaves quite a mark or impression. *Selfishness* is the stubborn person's form of pride. It works off of the ego and vanity of the stubborn person.

Stubborn people take pride in what appears to be selfless giving, when in reality, there is usually a self-serving motive behind it. The main motive behind this flurry of giving, besides the good feeling it provides, is often to receive the desired love or approval. They *want* people to exalt them in order to feel needed, understood, and important. Selfishness rears its ugly head in this nature after attempts of love and approval are not properly returned. This makes this type of person feel used and unappreciated. This is when selfishness becomes offended.

Offense produces frustration, which is verbally expressed by *words* that are followed by strong *attitudes*. These words are complaints or excuses that will escalate the momentum of selfishness. Selfishness begins to *emphasize* self blatantly. Such an emphasis becomes an appetite that cannot be satisfied. This inability to quiet selfishness and to keep it from exploding often causes frustration in those who are trying to contend with it.

Eventually, selfishness will build such a case in the stubborn person's mind that it begins to see and define the lack of response as treacherous and a form of betrayal. Due to the fact that their touchy emotions are taking center stage in their world, stubborn people take everything personally; therefore, in their mind everything is directed at them. They perceive betrayal as personal rejection. This will create the disguise of selfishness: that of the martyr syndrome.

As a martyr, the stubborn person becomes a suffering victim with an attitude. This bleeding, wounded victim may display self-pity and sarcasm. The end of this cycle is *depression*.

Overcoming

Those who are stubborn by nature must go through a *gold* process. This is where God allows friction in their world to sift or separate them from their unending excuses. This friction causes confusion and brings them to a point of total frustration. God wants stubborn people to realize they cannot handle life on their terms. All of their means of trying to substantiate their worth proves to be disappointing and depressing. These individuals must realize that they are only justified at the point of the blood of Jesus. This justification can only occur through repentance and faith.[1]

---

[1] Luke 13:5; Romans 4:5; 5:18

Stubborn people must learn to discipline their emotions and not their environment. This means they must first come under the control of the Holy Spirit. The Holy Spirit creates an attitude of meekness. This meekness produces self-control or temperance in the soul area.[2]

Self-control is very important for a stubborn person because they judge reality according to feelings rather by than the Word of God. Once the emotions are lined up with the Word of God, the stubborn person will have stability in their reality and world. If the emotions come under control, then the impulsive drive, persistence, and loyalties will be channeled in the right way.

It is also important for stubborn people to not take everything personally. They need to keep in mind that the world does not revolve around them. Much of what is happening around them is the evidence of human nature in operation, and not a personal affront against them. They must learn to discern between such matters by getting past touchy feelings, and properly discern what is going on in their environment.

Another trait that must be disciplined is the *stubborn* wall. Stubborn people must be careful about where they erect their wall. They need to be stubborn towards and for the things of God, but never in relationship to personal pride.

Selfishness must be mortified through neglect. It is hard for stubborn people to identify their pride because they are so giving. The test does not lie with outward actions, but inward motives.[3] The motives constitute selfishness; therefore, stubborn people need to rightfully discern their motives to avoid self-justification and delusion.

Stubborn people must mortify their standards or they are in danger of becoming bigoted, self-righteousness, dogmatic, and

---

[2] Galatians 5:22-23
[3] Proverbs 16:2

opinionated. Their unusually high standards are not realistic or obtainable. Ultimately, these standards will box this individual into a narrow, judgmental, self-centered world that becomes the means by which stubborn people judge all matters, including God.

The Word tells us God's ways are not the standards of the stubborn person. These standards may be high and rigid, but God does not ordain them. These narrow rulers become burdens too great to bear, as they comprise a yoke too heavy to carry. These people need to exchange their standards with Jesus' yoke and burden.[4]

Stubborn people must give up their need to be loved by others and allow the love of God to fill up that insatiable vacuum. The desire to find approval from others can prove to be a grave snare.[5] Because of this desire, many stubborn people accept ungodly relationships in order to get this need met. It is a dangerous trap.

These people must learn how to discern between conviction and condemnation to properly confront their guilt. The Holy Spirit convicts in order to bring a person to forgiveness and restoration, while Satan condemns. In condemnation, there is no hope for forgiveness and restoration, just hopelessness and the dread of future judgment.

Confrontation

Stubborn people operate according to a consistent cycle. It is easy to observe them and discover this cycle. The key to effectively entering in with stubborn people is one's ability to recognize this cycle and enter in at the right time.

Due to the emotional roller coaster of a stubborn person, it may appear difficult to determine when these people are actually in their cycle or whether they are venting emotions in order to keep

---

[4] Isaiah 55:8-9; Matthew 11:28-30
[5] Proverbs 29:25; 1John 4:16-19

things in perspective. If they are venting emotions because the frustration has built up in them, allow them to vent. Avoid getting in their face because you will be causing greater frustration.

To discern if a stubborn person is in their cycle, test their spirit. There is a decisive attitude behind these people's emotional momentum. Emotional venting comes in outbursts that indicate the person is working their way through the emotional maze, but in the stubborn cycle, it expresses itself in complaining. Complaining is different from the form of explanation and reasoning that often takes place in venting. Complaining is the means for this person to work up their emotional momentum in order to justify reactions.

If the stubborn person is working their way up into an emotional lather, you must effectively confront them at the point of *frustration*. The stubborn person will emotionally run over you past this point. The key is to get them to recognize what truly ails him or her. This could be interrupted plans or hurt feelings that have been stuffed. Due to a stubborn person's ability to stuff points of frustrations and hurts, they may run you around, but you need to continue to bring them back to reality. Eventually, the source of their agitation will be revealed. Once a stubborn person can get the source out in the open, it can be resolved, stopping the cycle and allowing the stubborn person to emotionally land.

Keep in mind that to enter in with stubborn people means you are emotionally entering in with their emotional struggles. If your motive is to calm this person so you can have peace, they will see through it and throw up their wall of mistrust. If you are condescending towards these people because of their emotions, or trying to manipulate them to get a desired effect, it will backfire on you. Godly confrontation is always about the other person and not for self-serving reasons. A right attitude in confrontation will ensure that the person's dignity will remain intact.

5

SELF-ASSURED NATURE

Self-assured people take pride in the idea that others cannot figure them out. They are *reserved* and will only let people in so far. They are also *unpredictable.* They can change in midstream when it comes to decisions, attitudes, and direction. This often causes confusion, chaos, and frustration for others.

Amazingly, self-assured people are easy to understand. The key to unlocking the mystery and confusion surrounding them comes down to something called *images.* Self-assured people have an image for every responsibility or role in their lives. For example, they will have an image for being a son or daughter, a sibling, friend, spouse, and parent. Each responsibility or demand requires a distinct, separate image. These different images are very detailed and demand perfection. Due to the need for perfection these people's greatest fear is *incompetence.*

These people can only maintain one image at a time. Tremendous frustration and anger arises when their different images begin to collide. You can actually witness them mentally scrambling to adjust their image according to the people that surround them. This conflict with images forces them to prioritize their images. The image that takes a back seat is usually that of the spouse.

Needless to say, the changing of image sends a mixed or confusing message to those who are contending with these individuals. Not only do they see the self-assured person change emphasis and attitude, but their course. This unpredictability causes confusion, insecurities, and conflict in the relationships of self-assured people.

In observing self-assured people, they use the confusion they create in their personal world to gain the upper hand over others. They use insecurities to lord over those in vulnerable positions, and conflict to control their space. In the end, it does not matter what kind of problems or conflicts they cause in their relationships, they will come out on top, or *justified* in their own sight.

This brings us to the self-assured motivation: pride. These people can display the very epitome of *pride*. Detailed concepts and high standards comprise their images. They can be very judgmental toward others. They not only personally operate according to images, but they have images for everyone and everything from their parents, spouses, and children to how their environment should look and function. When they encounter any inconsistency in any of these areas, they will become very judgmental and critical. In most cases, if one thing is out of order, they will zero in on the discrepancy while ignoring that which is right.

Their reactions to such discrepancies are often manifested in *cruelty*. They become very cutting or demeaning in their remarks. In their mind the situation is obvious to any thinking person; therefore, there will be no excuse for any inconsistency, and judgment will be rendered and demanded.

Self-assured people have a *lawyer's mind*. Each discrepancy is added to their list of offenses. This list can be literally written on various items, such as a piece of paper, on a calendar, or simply mentally erected in their minds.

These people have a *reservoir of anger*. When the reservoir is filled up, they will feel justified in taking actions against the culprit. Violence, cruelty, and mocking in various proportions are justified. It is not unusual for these people to shred those "culprits" whom they have a list against into hundreds of condescending pieces with their "list of evidence." Even though they leave their victims devastated, they feel justified. This justification makes them indifferent to the fruits of their personal actions, while changing their image makes them believe themselves to be guiltless of all wrongs committed by their previous expressions of anger, cruelty, and indifference.

Changing image simply means the person will change present reality. The image these people change into is either the "*good guy*" image or the one of a *victim* due to others' incompetence or injustice. Both the justification and image keep the self-assured person from ever being called to personal *accountability*. After all, their actions are justified, and due to the present image, they are not accountable for actions that occurred under another image.

Unless self-assured people have integrity at the point of their images, they can be good liars, especially to themselves. They will delude themselves by believing that their images truly represent their character and reality.

As you can see, images are everything to the self-assured person. However, these images are a means of hiding something. What are these images concealing? In fact, if you confront them, they will erect two walls to protect that hidden part of self from discovery.

The *first* wall is an *emotional wall*. When images begin to fail the situation, mass confusion hits the self-assured person. This confusion implies that this person's world is out of control. This will cause frustration that can express itself in an outburst of wailing or tears of *self-pity*. At the end of this wall is fear of incompetence, which immediately turns into anger. This anger is expressed in the second wall: that of *pride*. The wall of pride proves to be a harsh *unyielding* wall. This is where you discover that this person refuses to be wrong at any point, regardless of how much evidence can be provided as to their guilt.

The refusal to be wrong causes this individual to come across as being *mule-headed*. The difference between being bullheaded and mule-headed is that those who are bullheaded push their way through situations. Those who are mule-headed cause a fuss, which results in conflict and chaos among others in their environment. This redirects the focus from them, and puts it elsewhere.

It takes everything within self-assured people to admit when they are wrong. They often operate in generalities when it comes to personal injustices that they are directing at others. This unwillingness to be found, or proven, wrong causes them to be *indecisive* in making decisions. In fact, they often cleverly manipulate others around them to make desired decisions for them. For example, they present self-serving options. As they discuss these options with you, they cleverly nudge or push you towards the most preferred choice with their *logic* and strong *attitudes*. In the end, you usually make the decision they desire. The logic behind this game is that if anything goes wrong, guess who is to blame?

What are these people hiding behind their images? There are two traits they are hiding. The first trait is their incredible pride. This pride expresses itself throughout the self-assured person's many other traits. Pride is the essence of self. Therefore, whenever you encounter the pride of any nature, you have come to the end of that person. Unless this pride has been replaced with integrity, there is no character or substance behind it. It is at this point that you find out how deep or shallow a person is. This reality is clearly brought out in the self-assured person who has not developed integrity. Past these people's images, they can prove to be shallow vacuums that have no substance. They have nothing of importance or significance to offer.

The second trait self-assured people are hiding is their *fierceness*. They are fierce people. This can be expressed and seen through their *anger*. This fierceness is the force behind hiding and protecting both their pride and images. It is the unrelenting source behind justification. It causes intimidation through strong *attitudes*.

These people control and manipulate by using their *attitudes*. They can communicate volumes without saying a word. When accused of something that has not been made obvious through word or deed, they can deny it, laugh it off, mock, or become angry at the perceived injustice. Because of the strength behind these attitudes, people do adjust to them to avoid encountering the self-assured person's fierceness and possible repercussions.

If a self-assured person does make a decision without proper perspective, anger or vengeance often inspire it. These people can be very *persevering* in situations where they plan to make a statement, get their way, or an upper hand in a matter. They often leave a path of self-destruction without considering the devastation or consequences.

Once a self-assured person pays the consequences for personal actions, they will immediately take on the victim image, and display *self-pity*. Self-pity is the manifestation of fake nobility and worldly repentance. This can be seen in the lives of Esau and Judas Iscariot. Worldly repentance will always express itself in tears, while blaming others or circumstances for personal actions. This approach falls short of true repentance.[1]

Confrontation

Self-assured people can be quite miserable in their existence. Needless to say, this misery finds company with those who have to live or contend with them. In fact, the more miserable they are, the stronger their attitudes will become and the more difficult they are to contend with. The struggle can become so great within

---

[1] Matthew 27:3-9; 2 Corinthians 7:10; Hebrew 12:15-17

these people that they can appear close to insanity, especially if they are constantly trying to adjust or change images.

Images can cause a lot of confusion and chaos. These people naturally believe that those around them should bow down, adjust, and worship their images. When their image does not get the desired response, these people will take offence on behalf of their image. Therefore, how can you get past the image to minister to the person?

Depending on whether you are trying to minister to them or confront them will determine the strategy you use. If you are ministering to them, you have to *recognize* their images in order to keep their walls down.

These people desire *recognition* for what they are trying to accomplish through their image. By recognizing the image that is the most important or prevalent at that time, you can discern what they are trying to accomplish in the situation or relationship. This will keep the walls down so you can address their rigid, unrealistic standards, and reason with their emotional side. The goal is to get them past their images to clearly see the fruits of their lives. These people must see the contrast between where they are and what they are striving for. This contrast will help them to realize that their standards are unrealistic and unobtainable. Such contrast is important for them to see that their unrealistic standards cause fear, frustration, and anger.

When in confrontation with a self-assured person, never argue with them. Since these people have a *lawyer's mind,* they perceive themselves to be *logical.* You will never win an argument with them because they have cleverly built a case against you in their minds that they will use to justify their deviant actions at your expense. They will use their "list" against you every time.

Self-assured people use their strong attitudes to draw people into their legalistic trap. The key is not to venture their way regardless of how pouty or moody they become. Leave them alone in their small, self-centered worlds and go about your business. Like the groundhog, they will eventually have to raise their heads out of their self-pity and come to you. This means they are coming to you on your terms. When they do, hold the line. In other words, make them responsible for their personal attitudes and actions no matter how much they try to throw the blame on you or others. Emphasize the fact that they are responsible for their own disposition and actions, and one day, they will stand before God and give an account for their ways and deeds.

This allows you to put up the contrast and declare that you will not take responsibility for them. Confrontation with self-assured people calls for firmness, authority, and brutal honesty. You cannot let them off the hook for one second, and you cannot move from off the line of truth until they realize that you are not budging. It is as though you must gain the necessary respect each time you confront them to silence the case they have collected against you or others.

Overcoming the Image

Pride is the main trait that the self-assured people must overcome. Since pride is the very essence of who they are, it can require an intense process. This is why these people's process is related to that of *gold* where it must be *boiled* to separate the precious material from the impurities that are mixed with it. This boiling process is not only intense, but it can be quite drawn out.

As a reminder, pride looses its influence through neglect.[2] This simply means it must be replaced with integrity, and then ignored when it raises its head to demand obedience. Integrity helps a person discern between reality and the façade that such images create.

---

[2] Matthew 16:22-26

It is important that self-assured people fill up the vacant area behind pride with character that is produced by integrity. As they allow character to be worked in them by the Holy Spirit, their fierceness will be disciplined and channeled. Once channeled, this fierceness can be directed towards the work of God. This will bring forth powerful leadership in the kingdom of God.

Self-assured people must get rid of their lists of offences they are keeping to justify their attitudes and actions towards others. These people not only keep lists against others who have offended them, but against themselves for imperfections in their lives. These lists are opposite of love and faith. Love proves a person is of God, while faith is the only thing that truly pleases Him.[3]

These people need to ask God to show them each of the lists that they have developed against others, as well as against themselves. These lists serve as seeds that will breed bitterness and unforgiveness. These two sins will end up breaking a pure heart and making a person into a judgmental, self-serving skeptic.

The self-assured person needs to discover their real potential in Christ. This will bring their fierceness and standards under the control of the Holy Spirit. Such discipline will enable self-assured people to reach their potential in the kingdom of God.

---

[3] 1 Corinthians 13:4-8; Hebrews 11:6; 1 John 4:15-21

6

STRONG-WILLED NATURE

The biggest struggle for the strong-willed person is to let go of control of their atmosphere or world. In fact, *losing control* is the greatest fear of this person. It creates intensity and fear that can completely drive them into destructive behavior patterns.

These people operate in *extremes*. Even though strong-willed people give you an impression that all is calm, behind the scenes they are emotionally like bouncing balls. This extreme environment can be seen in their personality and atmospheres as well. For example, they can be very outgoing or very quiet. They can have a very orderly environment or they can live with an abundant amount of clutter. Either way, they are usually cognizant of what is affecting their world.

Strong-willed people are *decisive*. They make decisions that become concrete lines. These lines serve as boundaries in which these people perceive they can confidently operate. These boundaries form *ideas* that seem factual. Since these people perceive themselves as possessing *facts*, they cannot fathom the possibility of being wrong. Everything to them is black or white, and any shades of gray are either ignored or discarded. When these lines or ideas are challenged, these individuals will *make themselves right* in their own eyes regardless of the validity of the challenges.

These people maintain control by lining everything up in their world. They are people of *action*. Although much of what they do can prove to be nothing more than a bluff, they have a very intense atmosphere around them that causes others to line up or carry out their ideas. In fact, people around them can be intimidated by the strength that seems to permeate their sphere.

Strong-willed people's ability to get things done makes them appear to be *dynamic.* This dynamic appearance gives the impression that they are fearless. A great deal of this has to do with their *sense of infallibility*. Due to their factual perception, they believe there is no way they could be wrong about the decisions they have made or the conclusions they have come to. Since they are right, success awaits them. This success is usually just a matter of getting others to see it their way. Their ability to intimidate and bluff their way through situations serves as a powerful means to get others to line up to their way of doing or thinking. In fact, some of these people can bulldoze others over with their intensity, their sense of who they think they are, and their dynamic abilities to take on the impossible.

This brings us to the strong-willed person's need. This individual needs to be recognized for who they are. This *recognition* is a form of respect. Without this respect, strong-willed people will display mistrust towards others or lack confidence in their relationship with others. Mistrust will cause the strong-willed person to put up their wall.

The wall of mistrust is comprised of all of the traits of the strong-willed person. This wall can prove to be very immovable, and can make this type of person appear *hardheaded* when trying to reason with them. It also gives this individual a sense of infallibility. And, when the wall is erected, it is to maintain control of their world. This form of protection hides the tremendous fear that often drives this person to be impulsive or rash. The catalyst that holds this wall together is the strong-willed person's form of pride.

Immovable Will

The strong-willed person has an iron-clad will. This will is tied up in their need to control, as well as their form of pride. It serves as an immovable barrier that this individual cannot get around no matter what is happening in their world.

Interestingly, strong-willed people can be motivated by any one of the three forms of pride. These different forms of pride are what bring distinction among those who are strong-willed. It is obvious what form of pride drives each strong-willed person because it will be extreme

Although strong-willed people appear to be strong, they can prove to be very *fragile*. This is obvious when they encounter confusion. Confusion means that reality is colliding with their world. Confusion is unacceptable and will not be tolerated by these people. It is at this point that you can begin to see how the will works in the strong-willed person.

When reality fails to fit within the ideas of strong-will people, they basically will ignore it as if it was a lie or discard it as silly, heretical, or unrealistic. This ability may maintain personal reality for a season until challenged again, but it causes hardship on those around them. It is the people around these individuals who must pick up the pieces or deal with the consequences of the strong-willed person's unwillingness to realistically confront challenging reality.

When reality catches up to the strong-willed person, it can cause tremendous self-pity. These people *avoid the emotions* of others because they feel that such emotions will confuse the issue. They often act as if they are afraid of others' emotions, or will not tolerate them because they consider such emotions to be nonsense. However, when these people lose control, they can be very emotional. In fact, they can be extreme in their emotional responses.

I have been shocked at these people's ability to adjust reality. In a way, they become clueless. This is a form of denial or fantasy. These people have an uncanny ability to actually turn off their minds to anything that will not fit within their concrete lines. It is not unusual for this person to ask the same question numerous times. When this happens, it simply means that they have not yet heard the desired answer. It is as if they are waiting for reality to adjust to their perception or conclusion to a matter.

Sadly, these people can lose a lot of credibility. People, who do not understand how the strong-willed nature processes reality, will question these people's intelligence, hearing, and mental functioning. Strong-willed people usually miss viable details that would change the present facts or situation. There are four possible reasons as to why they miss such details: 1) These details may not fit within their lines; 2) they are considered insignificant in light of present circumstances; 3) there is too much activity going on in their environment, causing a state of confusion; and/ or 4) they assume others will take care of the details as they continue to confront greater issues. If these individuals do not have integrity, they will bluff their way through situations they do not understand because of their concrete lines and need to control.

Overcoming

Strong-willed people will be taken through a *diamond* process. The diamond starts out as a piece of coal. It appears as if it has worth, but coal is a piece of material that is ready to be consumed in the fire. On the other hand, the diamond represents a precious jewel that will be established in extreme heat and pressure. This means that a strong-willed person will go through an extreme process to ensure that they cease to be a piece of coal ready for judgment, and become a diamond that is being made ready to reach its potential.

These people often find themselves in extreme situations because they are not sensitive to what is happening in their reality. Because of their immovable lines, they have very limited vision, leaving them open to fall into Satan's various snares.

The real battle for strong-willed people begins with their will. They must exchange their iron-clad will for the will of the Father. This is very difficult since pride and control is mixed up in it. The will of the strong-willed person must be submitted before their *lines* can be properly adjusted or disciplined according to God's purpose. As long as the will is intact, these individuals' lines remain immovable. Once the lines can be adjusted, these people can be lined up to God's will and purpose.[1]

Strong-willed people must mortify their *obsession to control or rule*. This strong desire exalts them as God in their life. This is idolatry that will cause rebellion and set them up for a fall. In order to put to death this obsession, they must give way to the control of the Holy Spirit. This means walking according to the Spirit and not their personal boundaries. The leading of the Holy Ghost will take away the hardness of their lines, and will bring tremendous liberty to them as they walk by faith according to the life of the Son of God that must be developed in them.[2]

Strong-willed people must keep in mind that they are not infallible. They must not take themselves too seriously. This reality will keep them humble enough that others may be able to warn or instruct them. I encourage strong-willed people to surround themselves with godly counselors or advisers whom they respect and trust.[3]

---

[1] Luke 22:42; John 4:34
[2] 2 Corinthians 3:17; Galatians 5:16-18
[3] Proverbs 11:14

These people must learn to challenge their focus. Their ideas keep them very limited from perceiving reality around them. They must discipline their attention to embrace reality. This will help them to properly respond to and function among those around them.

In many cases, these people will surround themselves with those who will see it their way, ridding themselves of possible challenge or instruction. Strong-willed people can view any challenge as disrespectful instead of a necessity to maintain checks and balances in their lives and decisions. Beware of such strong-willed people because they harbor fragile egos due to fear, and are untrustworthy because there is no integrity or character.

Strong-willed people need to keep in mind that becoming a diamond is just part of the process. They must not only be completely changed from their lesser state to reach their potential, but they must be cut and polished. This process symbolizes their need to maintain a complete dependency on God to ensure that the remaining extreme traits of their nature will be properly disciplined and channeled for the glory of God.

Confronting the Diamond

Strong-willed people demand respect and shun emotions. If respect is missing, they will discard you as an insignificant nuisance. They want the facts, and in their book, emotions confuse the issue. In fact, avoid anything to do with feelings. Even the statement, "I feel this way about something," can be a big turn off to the people of this nature.

The main thing those who contend with strong-willed people must determine is what constitutes respect to these individuals. First of all, showing any fear or intimidation is not considered respect, but a weakness. A person must not only show respect to the strong-willed person, but also have their respect. The way you gain respect from this nature is to drop all emotions and signs of weakness.

If you have their respect, *look them in the eyes*. These people like eye contact. In their initial meeting with you, they size you up on the basis of whether you make eye contact with them. This is hard for other natures who may feel intimidated by them, but is vital if you are going to have any authority to speak into their lives.

Once you have their attention, firmly and decisively give them the facts. Avoid any type of explanation or rhetoric. You will immediately lose them. Keep it to the point and then back off. These people will make up their mind. Do not take it personally if they fail to respond to your warning or advice. If these people love God, it will be up to Him to confirm and adjust their lines.

In Review

Let us now compare the differences between these four natures. You will be able to see how distinct they are from each other. The differences are simple, yet they are far reaching when it comes to how each nature responds in crises and in their relationship to God and others. Consider the following table on the next page.

TRAITS	SUB-MISSIVE	STUBBORN	SELF-ASSURED	STRONG-WILLED
PROCESS	Pearl	Gold/Sifting	Gold/Boiling	Diamond
REBELLION	Withdraws	Justify (Front Door)	Justify (Back Door)	Make it Right
RESPONSES	Analytical	Impulsive	Unpredictable	Decisive
CHARACTER	Sweet	Personable	Reserved	Extreme
CONTROL	Words	Word/Attitudes	Attitudes/Actions	Actions
APPROACH	Persevere	Persistent (Aggressive)	Persistent (Logical)	Dynamic
PERCEPTION	Wise	Practical	Logical	Factual
PRIDE	Conceit	Selfishness	Pride	Any of the Three Forms of Pride
WALL	Fear	Stubborn	Emotional/Pride	Infallibility
NEED	Acceptance	Emotional Love	Recognition for their accomplish-ments	Recognition for who they are

7

REALITY VS. PERCEPTION

Each nature perceives themselves as being reasonable and realistic in their conclusions about present reality. In fact, each of these natures cannot perceive how they could be wrong about any matter they have carefully considered. This conclusion is in opposition to the words of Isaiah who declares that man's thoughts are not God's thoughts.[1]

God's thoughts consist of simple truths that are profound. The profound aspect of God's truths often causes people to complicate them in order to understand them. This complication actually is what perverts or defiles the truths of God. It is at this stage that man begins to hold the truth in unrighteousness, which is considered a serious offence in the Bible.[2]

Regardless of what nature a person may be, they are born with a selfish disposition. Unchallenged, selfishness always gives way to the lust of the flesh, the pride of life, and the lust of the eyes. When selfishness reigns, the pride of life is the motivation that reigns supreme when it comes to a person's perception. Pride perverts present reality and adjusts it according to personal conclusions. This pseudo reality often avoids personal accountability and responsibility, and falls short of coming to the truth of Jesus Christ.[3]

---

[1] Isaiah 55:8-9
[2] Romans 1:18
[3] John 14:6

People look to self to understand the workings and happenings of the world around them, rather than looking to God. The Apostle Paul talked about the unregenerate mind in Romans 8:6, "For to be carnally minded is death; but to be spiritually minded is life and peace."

Romans 12:2 states that the mind must be transformed. Transformation of the mind by the Holy Spirit will produce the mind of Christ. God is the only one who can bring a correct perspective to a person, but few ever take into consideration their need to have their minds transformed. They fail to believe that they know in part and see through a glass (flesh) darkly. They believe that God gave them a brain to find solutions. This conclusion causes them to lean on their own understanding.[4] Looking within for the answer causes introspection. Introspection points to a self-centered perspective.

Amazingly, people are surprised when they find out that their conclusions are not trustworthy and far from the truth that can make them free. They cannot fathom how their way of processing information could be far from reality. Even though there are Scriptures that warn each of us of the extent of our intellectual arrogance, we apply them to other people.[5] This makes us indifferent to our reality. We quickly judge others' conclusions as being ridiculous, without realizing that we are making that evaluation according to our own perverted conclusions.

In dealing with people, you will find that their reality hinders the work of God in their lives to bring them to restoration. They will often insist on their reality regardless of the fruit that is being produced in their relationships. They will deem other people's perceptions as being ridiculous and out of touch, while maintaining the reasoning behind their reality.

---

[4] Proverbs 3:5-7; 1 Corinthians 13:9, 12; Philippians 2:5
[5] John 8:32-36; Romans 12:3; 1 Corinthians 10:12; Galatians 6:3

It is important for each person to understand how they process information. Conclusions outside of God's perspective leave people in despair, disillusionment, depression, and delusion.

Consider the following diagram:

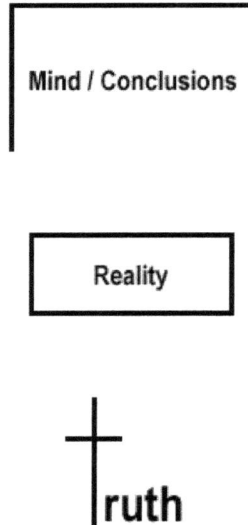

```
┌─────────────────────┐
│                     │
│  Mind / Conclusions │
│                     │
└─────────────────────┘


   ┌───────────────┐
   │    Reality    │
   └───────────────┘


          ┼
          │ruth
```

Notice how you cannot come to truth without facing present reality. Sadly, most people refuse to face reality, and will go into their own minds to create a desired reality. The problem with this scenario is that others will not share in that perception. They have their own perceptions. As a result, others are always challenging the personal reality of these individuals. This causes frustration, resentment, anger, and bitterness.

Let's consider how each nature changes their reality. This is important because people insist on their personal reality, while letting life pass them by. They either live in the past or the future, but few ever properly deal in the present.[6]

---

[6] For a more detailed presentation on how people handle reality, see *Battle for the Soul*, by the same author.

Submissive people use their *analytical* process to come to an understanding about a situation. They actually run around in their different compartments to collect the necessary data to consider all of their possible options. When they have combined all of the information together, they make a decision. To these individuals, this conclusion seems *wise* and unshakable. They conclude that this is the *way things should be*, and there is no way that they can be wrong since they have considered all of the pertinent information.

These people underestimate the depth of darkness that is attached to their intellectual conceit. Conceit perverts reality and truth. It is a product of human wisdom. Human wisdom is earthly, sensual, and devilish. It may be based on experience and common sense, but it lacks God's perspective. All the submissive person has succeeded in doing is *recreating* their own reality. These individuals can become wise in their own conceits as they fail to connect with the reality around them.[7]

God does not choose human wisdom to reveal His wisdom. The Apostle Paul made this statement in regards to how God will expose the vanity of the wisdom that is inspired by this present world in 1 Corinthians 1:27, "But God hath chosen the foolish things of the world to confound the wise."

God uses the means of simplicity, not intellectual evaluation to reveal His truths. The Apostle Paul expressed real concern about those who complicate the truths of God, "But I fear, lest by any means, as the serpent beguiled Eve through his subtlety, so your minds should be corrupted from the simplicity that is in Christ" (2 Corinthians 11:3).

The analytical ways of the submissive person will fail to solve the problem. When understanding or resolutions fail them, they

---

[7] Romans 12:16; James 3:13-18

will begin to create a rut in their mind. This rut will develop into a pit of dramatization and depression.

Consider the following diagram:

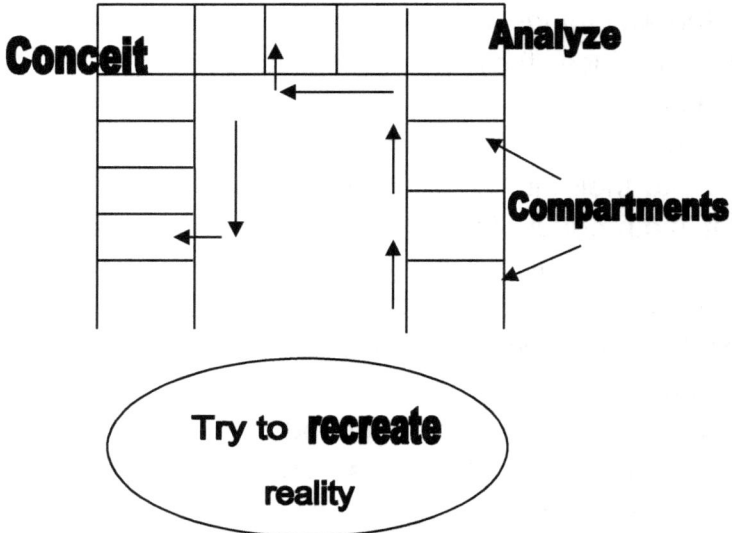

Conceit   **Analyze**

Compartments

Try to **recreate** reality

Stubborn people believe themselves to be *practical* about how they view and approach life. Information is not put into a mental box like the submissive person. Rather, they have an uncanny ability to pull it out of the hat when needed. The reason for this is because their information is often interpreted by how something makes them feel. Emotions and their environment make up a big part of how these people process information. Since these people can feel deeply about something, they perceive it as truth.

Standards are also used by stubborn people to process information. These standards serve as a means of bringing discipline to their environment. They determine *how something should be*. These rulers are a product of pride. In their mind, these standards are practical, even though they grow in requirements and demands. Eventually, these standards become harsh and unobtainable. If not kept in the right perspective, these standards will cause the stubborn person to become unloving, unrealistic, judgmental, skeptical, and unreasonable.

When you combine standards with emotions, you will have individuals who will *adjust* their environment to fit the reality they perceive is right according to how they feel. This reality can be aggressive to those who have to deal with it. It can be opinionated, dogmatic, and immovable when challenged.

The Apostle Paul tells us that God has chosen, "…base things of the world" (1 Corinthians 1:28). Base things seem unlikely and impractical, but they make up a burden that is light and reachable by those who are sincere in heart. They will bring individuals under the yoke of Jesus, rather than serve as an unbearable yoke to those who are struggling with the demands of life.[8]

Consider the following diagram:

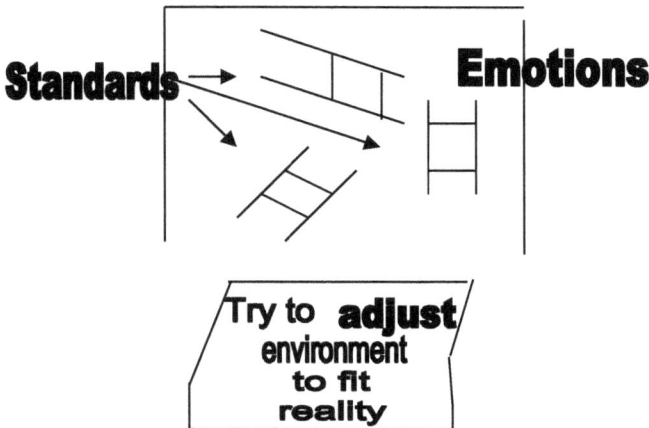

Standards → **Emotions**

Try to **adjust** environment to fit reality

---

[8] Matthew 11:28-30

Self-assured people perceive themselves to be *logical* in their conclusions. These conclusions are based on their *images*. These images are forever trying to get others to *adjust* to their perception of reality. This is different from the stubborn person who tries to adjust their environment to their reality.

These images are made up of tough *standards* that demand perfection. They determine *the way things must be*. The problem with these images is that if self-assured people perceive themselves as failing to live up to a particular image, they simply change to another image. Each image becomes their reality. Meanwhile, they expect others to adjust to their image and confirm this reality. Since these images constantly change, reality becomes fickle and confusing to those who are contending with this person. They often do not know which way to turn. They realize the person has changed in midstream, but they see it as hypocrisy, rather than the "changing of the guard."

When people fail to adjust to the reality of a self-assured person, their reservoir of anger begins to fill up. This reservoir will eventually allow them to adjust their reality to justify any ungodly or immoral actions towards those who fail to reinforce their images. This can be a frightening reality to those around this type of individual, because this person is not only unrealistic, but also unreachable. All the reasoning in the world will be shot down by their list of justifications.

The Apostle Paul tells us that God has chosen, "..things which are despised" (1 Corinthians 1:28). God uses what many would consider contemptible or far from perfection. In the end, His character and truth will be upheld, not surface images that show contempt towards those who refuse to worship them.

Consider the following diagram.

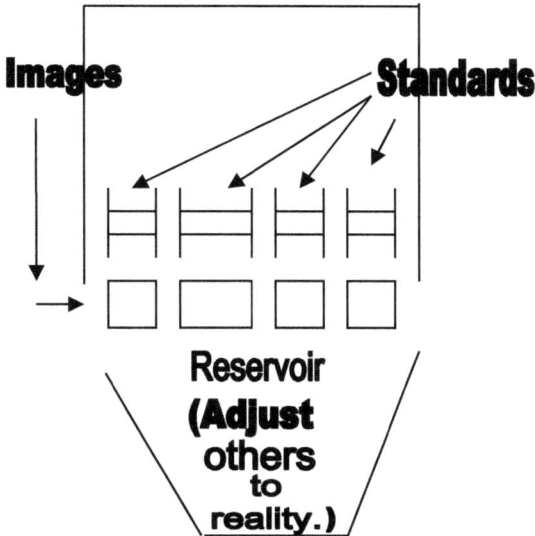

Strong-willed people *reshape* reality to fit within their *ideas*. These ideas establish *how things will be,* and are made up of lines of facts. These people perceive themselves as having all the necessary facts to determine the proper reality. Since they conclude that what they know is true, these lines become cemented into their perception. They actually use the lines to reshape all information to their ideas. If any information does not fit within these lines, it is often ignored or discarded. As previously stated, these people can ask the same question over and over again. It is their way of seeing if the information has been adjusted in any way, so that they can fit it into their world. Apparently, they must conclude that if they ask the same question enough times, that particular reality will change, and line up to what they perceive to be the only acceptable reality.

It is amazing to watch these people reshape their reality. They consider all the angles in which they can approach a subject. They use each approach as if they are trying to herd or corral you into their neat, controlled reality. Their attempts can become elaborate and manipulative. Sadly, this is what they do with their understanding of God as well. If they run out of angles, then they become confused and resort to intimidation.

The Apostle Paul tells us that God has chosen, "…things which are not, to bring to nought things that are" (1 Corinthians 1:28). God chooses things that seem insignificant and unimportant to bring forth His truth and message. Strong-willed people need to realize that reality does not rest within their concrete ideas, but in simple truths that will not always fit into their perception.

Consider the following diagram

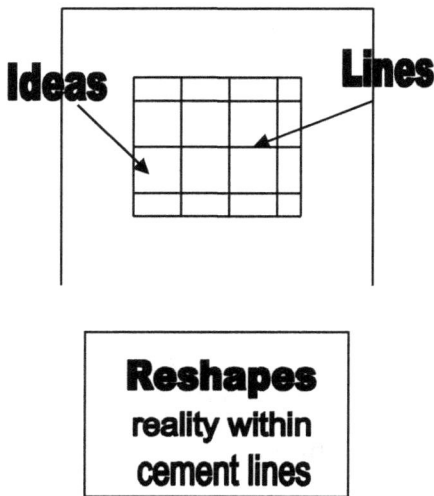

Each nature is in search of a particular reality. Much of this search has to do with vainglory. This vainglory is about receiving recognition for wisdom or intelligence, and in personally determining what constitutes reality and truth. For the submissive, they desire *wisdom,* while stubborn people want to be *righteous* about their decisions. The self-assured seeks after *perfection,* while the strong-willed desires *completion* and *certainty*. Sadly, what each of these natures do not realize is that their particular form of reality can only be found in a relationship with God through Jesus Christ, as they yield completely to His Lordship.

The Apostle Paul brought this out in 1 Corinthians 1:29-31, "That no flesh should glory in his presence. But of him are ye in Christ Jesus, who of God is made unto us wisdom, and righteousness, and sanctification, and redemption: That, according as it is written, he that glorieth, let him glory in the Lord." Jesus serves as wisdom to the submissive and is the essence of righteousness for the stubborn. To the self-assured, He is sanctification who points to perfection through servitude. For the strong-willed, He is the point of redemption that is certain and complete for all who will come to Him on His terms.

Man's desire to glory in self, keeps him from realizing his life in Christ. His desire to control his reality, keeps him from coming to truth. His insatiable need to reign prevents him from reaching his potential in Christ.

What are you seeking after? How far away from truth are you? Is your perception worldly or heavenly? If you are operating outside of Jesus, you are already on a dead-end road.

8

COUNTERFEIT REPENTANCE

The study of man's fallen condition confirms God's evaluation of it, which is found in His Word. It is easy to quote Scripture concerning the sin that plagues man's relationship with God, but few ever receive a personal revelation of their own depravity. Until a person does receive such a revelation, they will maintain there is something good or beneficial in their very person that is worth salvaging. As long as individuals maintain this delusion, they will not see the need to totally sell out to God.

Total abandonment comes out of brokenness before God. This brokenness is a result of coming face to face with this depravity. As one discovers the depths of their fallen condition, they become crushed under the weight of hopelessness. Once a person comes to this point, they can do one of two things: repent or perish.

Jesus said in Luke 13:3, "I tell you, Nay: but, except ye repent, ye shall all likewise perish." One cannot get to heaven without repenting. This is why it is God's will that all come to repentance to avoid spiritual separation and ruin.[1]

Repentance is a simple matter of a complete change. It means turning from the present way of thinking, feeling, and being, towards God's way of thinking and responding. Sadly, the selfish

---

[1] 2 Peter 3:9

disposition complicates repentance, preventing people from coming to true repentance. People do not know how to repent because it does not involve a formula, but humility and brokenness that is contrary to selfishness. In fact, each nature provides a counterfeit repentance that can delude its victim and somewhat deceive others. But, eventually it is exposed as a counterfeit because there is no evidence of fruits that are fit for repentance.[2] This simply means there is no inward change of character that would be evident in real repentance.

2 Corinthians 7:10 talks about the two types of repentance that are in operation, "For godly sorrow worketh repentance to salvation not to be repented of: but the sorrow of the world worketh death." Real repentance involves godly sorrow. Sorrow points to heaviness. For those who have godly sorrow, this heaviness is not only great, but also is repulsed towards sin and an unacceptable attitude towards deviant conduct. People with godly sorrow will come to the cross of Jesus, seeking the means of rolling off this heaviness through forgiveness and cleansing; thereby, resulting in reconciliation, restoration, and salvation.[3]

Worldly sorrow expresses itself in personal penitence, tears of self-pity, and the victim syndrome.[4] This type of sorrow is seeking personal recognition by showing how much it is suffering for deserved consequences. This suffering is fake nobility that holds onto its personal dignity regardless of the extent or damage that personal sin has cost God and others. It is a form of pride with the appearance of repentance, but it refuses to submit to the humbling work of the cross of Jesus. As a result, it leads to death or separation from God.

To clearly see the contrast between these two types of repentance, you can study the parable of the Prodigal Son in Luke

---

[2] Matthew 3:8
[3] Matthew 11:28-30
[4] Hebrews 12:16-17

15:11-32, and Judas Iscariot's handling of his betrayal of Jesus in Matthew 27:1-5. The prodigal son recognized the condition he was in after squandering his inheritance and wallowing with the pigs. He concluded that being a servant in his father's house was greater than his present situation. He humbled himself, ceased from his way of thinking and doing, and went back home. Before his father, he acknowledged his sin and was willing to accept the consequences of his action by becoming a servant. He knew he was not worthy of his status as a son. His repentant attitude and action caused his father to rejoice, as well as allowed him to restore him as a son.

Judas Iscariot displayed worldly sorrow after he realized the gravity of his actions of betraying Jesus. He went to the religious leaders and confessed his error to them, rather than to the one he had offended. He admitted that he had betrayed an innocent man. This declaration still showed that Judas did not believe Jesus Christ's declaration about His true identity. Jesus was not just an innocent man; He was and is the perfect Son of God, the promised Messiah. Judas failed to see that his sin was against God. Repentance involves coming into agreement with God's evaluation about a matter. When the leaders failed to absolve Judas for his actions, he threw the coins down, ran out and hung himself. At every point, we see where Judas sought man's absolution rather than God's forgiveness. In the end, he took matters into his own hands and hung himself.

Obviously, godly repentance turns to God, while worldly sorrow turns to self or others to make it right. Godly sorrow takes full responsibility for personal actions, while worldly repentance becomes noble in the situation. Worldly sorrow throws a bone by confessing wrongs, while maintaining the same ungodly mannerisms, attitudes, and practices. Godly repentance will turn to God with an open heart in humility and confession, seeking reconciliation with Him. Such repentance will cause the person to cease from ungodly attitudes and actions; and become changed in their disposition, as they submit to discipline.

True to his deceptive form, fallen man's tendency is to always resort to worldly sorrow. It cleverly counterfeits repentance in such a way that those who are trying to come to repentance often mistake it for godly sorrow on their part. This delusion causes these individuals to walk in deception about their life before God and the destructive path they are still on.

Worldly repentance expresses itself differently among the four natures. Each nature has its own form of repentance and delusion. In order for people to overcome their sin, they must understand how they counterfeit repentance.

Submissive people withdraw into their minds. They run around in each compartment trying to figure out where they went wrong. If they discover that they were indeed foolish, they begin to go through mental whippings. This is a way of chastising themselves. In this process, they may confess outwardly the gravity of their actions, but they are busy trying to devise a means by which to avoid the same scenario in the future. This is a type of *flattery* that appears sincere outwardly, but is a form of deception.

The problem is that since submissive people work it all out in their mind, they perceive it as repentance. They can even acquire a peace about the situation, but the peace is a result of them coming to an understanding about it and not because they have repented. Since they have a personal understanding about it, they feel they have resolved it, but this resolution is temporary. Although they may have *complied* outwardly, their patterns and fruits remain unchanged. Each time they encounter failure in the same area, their patterns of repentance and rebellion get shorter. In spite of the obvious failure that comes from seeking resolution in their mind, they fail to come to the foot of the cross of Jesus seeking forgiveness, cleansing, reconciliation, and restoration.

Stubborn people's worldly sorrow can involve two different responses. First, they will adjust their standards even higher as a means to discipline themselves. This discipline will supposedly keep them from committing the same unforgivable error. Or, they will resort to emotionally whipping themselves by deprivation or some form of abuse to resolve their guilt. This whipping can be intense, but it is their way of getting back into God's good graces. In a way, it is the same as *reformation*. However, such reformation is surface, thereby, misleading. Therefore, it is not unusual to witness them in the same repentant process, while justifying the same wrongdoings at the expense of others.

Such justification wins out, and they begin the process of putting their world back together. The problem is that these people often live in a fantasy world. They do not deal in reality concerning their relationships with others. This is where their incredible ability to *con* themselves, as well as others, comes into play. The attitudes and problems that have brought them to the state of incredible guilt, rejection, or failure remain intact, but their fantasy keeps them from facing this reality. Reality eventually challenges them and they fall back into the same patterns.

Each time stubborn people find themselves in the same pattern, it causes them to be overwhelmed with greater condemnation. When the condemnation becomes too great, they will find themselves being pushed by guilt and fear. For some to rid themselves of these intense feelings, they fine-tune their justification in such a way that they begin to operate in delusion, anger, obsession, and insanity.

If stubborn people would come to the cross of Jesus, they could calm the intense feelings of guilt and fear by embracing His forgiveness. But, if their standards are reigning, these people feel they cannot come to the cross until they right the situation. This gives Satan an inroad to lie, deceive, or condemn them even more. They could silence the many lies of Satan by allowing

Jesus' blood to justify them. They could ultimately know liberty from condemnation as they receive by faith in order to experience His abiding mercy and grace.

Self-assured people fake repentance by adjusting the standards behind their images. This is nothing more than a *performance* on their part that gives the outward appearance that they have changed, while *concealing* the reality that nothing has changed in their disposition. As they adjust their reality, they begin to *delude* themselves as well as others about what is genuine. They are still hiding their deviations behind masks, while holding on to their right to maintain their lists, rights, and games of control and manipulation.

In most cases these people will not admit when they are wrong. I had a self-assured person admit that she will apologize for something she is not guilty of, rather than take responsibility when she is wrong. Even in the area of accountability, these people will play games with you. They can afford to "owe" up when they are not in the wrong because they can give an impression of being noble, but will refuse to admit any incompetence in situations where personal wrongdoing is obvious. In my encounters with these people, they will admit they are wrong in a generic sense, but will fall short of ever taking accountability for individual sins.

Jesus talked about taking away the cloak to reveal sin, and even declaring secret words from the housetop.[5] Obviously, sin cannot be hidden. The Light of the world will reveal all secret thoughts and sins. It would be wise for people to quit trying to conceal sins and bring them to the cross in humility and brokenness in order to experience forgiveness and restoration. As Proverbs 28:13 states, "He that covereth his sins shall not

---

[5] Luke 12:2-3; John 15:22

prosper: but whoso confesseth and forsaketh them shall have mercy."

Strong-willed people work worldly sorrow from two angles. The first angle is that they will fit their interpretation of a discrepancy into their lines. Once this happens, the issue becomes automatically resolved even though there is no change. The second approach is that they will appear to agree up front that it may not be right, while maintaining their lines. Basically, this is throwing a bone for the purpose of getting a person off their back and winning confidence. This is a form of outward *conformity*, but its goal is to maintain control or get control of a situation. It is all part of their game plan. In addition, if it does not work, they will try to bluff or intimidate a person to line up to their reality.

The reason strong-willed people avoid genuine repentance is because they must lose control and come under the authority of Jesus. Therefore, their worldly sorrow strives to maintain personal control to conform people or situations to their atmosphere.

The predominant fruits of worldly sorrow are self-righteousness and self-pity. If people manage to succeed in changing their worlds around them through the fallacy of counterfeit repentance, they become very self-righteous. After all, they managed to change the situation in their own power. Therefore, these individuals have a right to glory in it and lord it over others.

The reality that one faces in genuine repentance is that only God can change the heart, disposition, and perception of a person. Godly repentance brings to focus the person's need for God's intervention to save them from the arrogance and delusion of self.

When worldly sorrow fails to get desired results, self-pity raises its ugly head. After all, each nature has striven hard to deal with, handle, or take care of their particular discrepancy. When they encounter an unresponsive response from others, they perceive themselves to be victims. They conclude people just do not understand their situation. This conclusion causes these souls to perceive themselves as an exception to the rule, and such hypocrisy ultimately exalts them above Scriptural accountability and reason.

There is one virtue that allows people to discern between these two forms of repentance: integrity. Integrity will honestly evaluate self according to personal fruits rather than personal opinions or fantasies. It will line up to God's evaluation of a matter, and will not be content until it is resolved before the throne of grace.

King David was a man who walked according to the integrity in his heart.[6] When he was confronted about his different failures, he never counterfeited repentance. He came to God, humbled himself, confessed his sins, and threw himself on His mercy. This is clearly revealed in his famous prayer of repentance found in Psalm 51.

Integrity has to be applied at certain points depending on a person's nature. For example, integrity must be applied at the end of a *submissive* person's conclusions. If integrity is reigning, the submissive person will conclude that they cannot trust their personal conclusions. The final analysis will be that they have been leaning on their own understanding, and that God's thoughts are much higher and beyond personal evaluation and comprehension.[6] This conclusion will take the intensity and reality out of this person's understanding and put the emphasis back on gaining God's perspective.

Stubborn people must apply integrity at the point of their overwhelming emotions. Emotions often create present reality for a stubborn person rather than the Word of God. These people must avoid giving in to the cycles of their emotions, and actually

---

[6] 1 Kings 9:4
[6] Proverbs 3:5; Isaiah 55:8-9

pull themselves up to consider what the Word of God says about a matter. This requires them to make a choice in the will area to seek out God's understanding by first disciplining their emotions. The key for the stubborn person is not to ignore or close down their emotions, but face their instability in discerning reality. These individuals must choose not to give in to the false reality they create by choosing to put their faith in God's Word.

Self-assured people must institute integrity up front before they give way to the false reality of their images to ensure godly repentance. They must recognize the hypocrisy and deception that each of their images create. They must hold each image lightly, and test themselves according to the fruit that is being manifested when they encounter challenges to their reality, as well as what they consider to be disrespect in relationship to their images and the adversity it creates.

Strong-willed people must apply integrity at the point of their motivation and lines. Few strong-willed people test their motivation behind their atmosphere, attitudes, and actions. They see themselves as being right and cannot imagine how they could be wrong. However, if the motivation or spirit, behind something is self-serving, or serves as a means of controlling others, it will be considered wrong and unacceptable to God. These individuals must realize their lines do not constitute a right spirit, nor do they establish reality.

It is vital for strong-willed people to test the spirit behind them, and allow God to adjust their lines to His way of doing. This means they must take their conclusions lightly until they can be properly tested. They must relinquish to God their need to control in order to ensure uprightness.

The question is this, have you come to real repentance, or are you operating in a counterfeit repentance? Have you properly applied integrity or are you walking in fake humility, personal justification, and self-delusion?

9

THE PROCESS

God's Word is quite clear. Christians must overcome. The message to the seven churches in Revelation 2-3 confirms that overcoming is not an option, but a requirement to possess all that God has for His people. Revelation 21:7 gives this promise, "He that overcometh shall inherit all things; and I will be his God, and he shall be my son."

As we have taken this journey through the fallen ways of man, it has become obvious that many people want to fake spiritual victory, rather than pay the price to know God. They want to put a cloak over sin, rehabilitate the old man (the flesh) while still placating its appetites, and subtly give way to the idolatry of pride by disguising it behind fake humility. Many such individuals are hoping they can slide into heaven without anyone discovering that they have been operating according to the ways of the flesh, instead of walking in righteousness. These people devise ways to take the path of least resistance, while giving the appearance of repentance, obedience, and sacrifice.

Sadly, this scenario is the epitaph of the fallen condition. Like the rich man in Luke 16, the old man seems to trip over that which seems insignificant, to only taste the reality of hell. Man is forever tripping over the filthy rags of his righteousness, the so-called insignificance of justified sins, and the compromise of the world. What seems petty or unimportant to the old man becomes the open door to spiritual ruin and defeat.

There are three things that the Word of God commands His people to overcome: the world, the flesh, and the devil. The world is capable of entangling people in its destructive web. This represents a challenge because the world consists of doing that which is *necessary*. The necessities of life are neither good nor evil, but they can be exalted improperly. Such exaltation will allow the needs and demands of the world to choke or drown out God's Word. These cares can clutter the real issues of life.[1]

A person who gives in to the world begins to lose perspective. Wants are viewed as needs, and life begins to consist of worldly possessions, rather than Christ. Eventually, the demands of the world grow to such proportions that they suck the spiritual life out of a person as they pervert what is holy, pure, and acceptable.

Jesus instructed His followers to not fear the world for He overcame it. Since believers' lives are hid in Christ, they do not have to fear the world or fall into its various traps. In fact, the solution to overcoming the world is for a person to grow in their testimony of Jesus. This maintains a growing relationship, ensuring a right focus and perspective.[2]

The flesh is the next predominant enemy of our souls. It serves as the main open door to spiritual oppression. The confusion with this area is that the flesh represents doing that which is *natural*. How could something that is so natural and brings such pleasure, be so wrong to God? It comes down to the harsh reality that the flesh defiles the things of God and results in spiritual death.[3]

Total abandonment from the dictates of the flesh is the means of overcoming it. This abandonment points to consecration. Consecration is where the person physically separates self from that which is unholy, for the purpose of emotionally and spiritually being separated unto God.

---

[1] Matthew 13:22; Luke 12:15; 2 Timothy 2:3-4
[2] John 16:33; 1 John 5:5; Revelation 12:11
[3] Romans 8:13

Separation unto God is the work of sanctification. It involves a cleansing. We already know that the blood of the Lamb cleanses believers. Revelation 12:11 reminds us that followers of God overcome with the blood of the Lamb. The blood of the Lamb points to a new covenant. This covenant allows us to be children of God. It sets us apart because a seal of identity is upon us, a heavenly inheritance awaits us, and the right to enter into the throne room without fear of judgment is before us. With this new covenant of redemption, we can walk in the light and experience fellowship with God and others.

The Holy Spirit is the One who does this inward, transforming work of sanctification. This ensures fellowship, growth, and victory over Satan. To ensure the work of sanctification, a person must submit to God. As they submit, priorities and focus change. Eventually, the ways of the flesh will become unnatural and repulsive, while the ways of God will be perceived as normal.

The final enemy that must be overcome is Satan. He causes activities that are *unnatural*. In fact, he pushes everything into extremes. Extremes of this nature cause oppression or bondage. Such bondage keeps a person from moving forward in their relationship with God. The three means of overcoming Satan are clearly stipulated in Revelations 12:11, "And they overcame him by the blood of the Lamb, and by the word of their testimony, and they loved not their lives unto the death."

Walking in the New Testament covenant will help Christians overcome the flesh. Properly applying God's Word will enable believers to overcome the world. By closing down these two avenues, Satan has no inroads. But, before these avenues can be dealt with, one must cease to love the life that is associated with the world around us.

The world and the flesh are associated with life as we know it. Jesus made this statement in Matthew 16:25, "For whosoever will save his life shall lose it: and whosoever will lose his life for my sake shall find it." Man's greatest desire and struggle is to maintain life as he knows or perceives it. This life is based on self, the flesh, and the values of the world. Self has rights, the flesh has its many wants (lusts), and the world has various counterfeits that cleverly replace the need for God. Such counterfeits are pagan and idolatrous.

People cling to this life because it offers happiness and seems so logical. However, Jesus stated that if people are not willing to lose life as they know or perceive it here, they will lose it all in the end—meaning their very souls.

Each nature must go through the process in order to lose the essence of identity of self to reach its potential in God. For example, *submissive* people find their identity in their ability to analyze. Eventually, their ability is proven incapable of changing the face of life as they fail to intellectually resolve problems. These unresolved problems begin to create *irritations*.

As submissive people file each fact away or ignore each problem, this combination creates a tidal wave that eventually catches up to them, leaving them foundering in a whirlpool of failure and despair. It is only after submissive people run out of options that they might look up from their pit of depression to seek God's perspective. As God surrounds them with His perspective, they start being formed as the *pearl* that He intends them to be.

Submissive people avoid coming to terms with the depravity of their fallen condition. They do this by running away from reality in their mind or wallowing in a world of fake nobility and self-pity. In their conceited way, they can create a reality that feeds their pride as they imagine how they would direct the world and the people around them. They will attempt to make their world comply through sweetness and diplomacy, and when they fail to accomplish this task, they translate it as failure. Instead of taking accountability, they will strive to maintain the dignity of their arrogance. They do this by hiding behind fake nobility or becoming a suffering victim.

Stubborn people must be separated from their *self-justification*. For this to happen, their environment must become overwhelming, out of control, and chaotic. Environment is practically everything to these people. In fact, the environment of a stubborn person will determine their identity. This environment reflects this type of person's emotional stability. The more chaos, the greater stubborn people attempt to control their environment. This will cause tremendous pressure for everyone who enters the stubborn person's world. They will feel the pressure to *reform* according to the stubborn person's expectations put upon them by complaints or attitudes. Even if people reform, the pressure continues to escalates due to the fact that there is something amiss in the inward environment of the stubborn person. Pressure of this type will produce a *sifting* or *friction* process.

Friction eventually wears down the resolve of the stubborn person. This process is capable of bringing the stubborn person to the end of self where either submission to God or emotional suicide, are the only two choices left. If God is allowed to have His way in this person, they will come forth as *gold* that is ready to be shaped for His work. Sadly, some stubborn people opt for emotional suicide where they close down and become zombies.

Self-assured people must be separated from their images. Images determine these people's ever-changing reality. They are always trying to get others to perform according to their images. However, people rarely perform, and life will not be adjusted, causing the process to either begin or escalate for these individuals. The process includes a *boiling* process of adversity that will eventually separate them from their various images to establish them in reality.

These people must be brought to the end of the fallacy of their images. Once they face the hypocrisy and fallacy of their images, one of three things will occur: 1) They will become angry and vengeful, 2) they will become apathetic with underlying anger and self-pity ready to erupt, or 3) they will develop integrity and come forth as pure *gold*.

Strong-willed people often give themselves no other choice but to experience the extreme process of a *diamond*. This extreme pressure comes when the strong-willed person loses control. The heat is turned up when others refuse to conform to this person's world and play their games of control. The more the struggle to control those in their world, the greater the process escalates until the strong-willed person is brought to a place of being in a fragile or vulnerable state. This state can drive these people into one of two directions: 1) Either they will go into total delusion about their spiritual condition, which brings them to the brink of destruction, or 2) they will be broken and forced to run into God.

Sadly, very few people accept the challenge of their process. They try to fake it or give the impression that they have paid the necessary price to become priceless heirlooms in God's kingdom. The problem is that there is no change, and when they pay the consequences, they groan and moan about how great the price is. The truth is, when one is truly paying the price to know God, it is not a source of great suffering, but one of great privilege and identification. In other words, there is no moaning or self-glorification, but an abiding peace in the reality of possessing in greater measures the precious treasure of heaven.

Jesus gave simple instruction to all of his disciples in Matthew 16:24 to ensure this process, "If any man will come after me, let him deny himself, and take up his cross, and follow me." Self-denial works within two avenues: 1) Not giving in to self and 2) obedience to what is right.

When a person refuses to give in to self, they will neglect the demands and vain imaginations of pride and submit to the work of the Holy Ghost. Such work points to abandonment to self, which is a form of consecration. Consecration allows one to submit to the work of sanctification that is done by the Holy Spirit.[4]

Self-denial is the first step because without it the selfish disposition in us will become a noble, suffering martyr when the cross is applied. The cross represents death. The flesh with its disposition must be put upon the cross daily.[5] As the flesh is daily mortified, a person becomes crucified to the influences of the world. The Apostle Paul confirmed this in Galatians 6:14, "But God forbid that I should glory, save in the cross of our Lord Jesus Christ, by whom the world is crucified unto me, and I unto the world."

Once self is denied and the personal cross applied, a person will have the discipline to follow Jesus. Some Christians believe that it is easy to follow Jesus, but they do so in foolish zeal and ignorance.[6] Eventually, they take detours or get ahead of Jesus. Godly discipline can only come by way of neglecting the essence of the pride of self and properly applying the cross to the "old man" in us.

Each nature has a different challenge when confronting self and applying the cross. For example, *submissive* people must neglect giving in to the arrogance of their conceits. They become so top heavy in knowledge that they forget to be realistic and sensitive to others, as well as the world around them. They eventually become so certain and deluded in their intellectual conclusions, they become fools.

They must cease from taking their conclusions seriously and seek after God's perspective. This means submissive people must apply the cross to their concepts or notions about what constitutes reality and *wisdom*. Application of the cross at this point will do

---

[4] Romans 15:16; 1 Peter 1:2
[5] Luke 9:23
[6] Romans 10:2-3

91

away with identity based on personal understanding, allowing them to seek identity in God's incredible wisdom.

Stubborn people must neglect the insatiable demands of their selfishness to control their environment to feel loved or on top of their emotional life. Controlling environment implies they have to get those in their environment to bow down to their perception and demands. The problem with this is as others react to the stubborn person's attempts to control their world, these unsuspecting individuals will begin to define or establish the stubborn person's identity. In other words, this identity will come down to how others make a stubborn person feel about themselves.

Once stubborn people discipline their emotions by neglecting their selfishness, they can apply the cross to their unrealistic standards. These standards serve as a form of personal *righteousness*, but they create tremendous yokes and burdens that are too harsh and cruel to bear. In fact, these unrealistic yokes and burdens make stubborn people critical, skeptical, and hard towards others who fail to agree or adhere to them.

Self-assured people must avoid giving in to realities established by their images. They must realize that these different realities do not constitute fruit, integrity, or truth, but a façade that keeps them from properly functioning in the world around them and in relationships. Ultimately, it will keep them from entering into the kingdom of God. By neglecting the demands of the different realities that are created by these images, they can effectively apply the cross to each of their images.

These people search for perfection in their images can only be realized in the work of *sanctification*. Sanctification can only take place when their images are properly dealt with. Therefore, it is important to mortify these images because they serve as the essence of self. They actually determine the variety of confusing and unpredictable identities these people interchange or display.

Strong-willed people must neglect the sense of infallibility created by their pride. In other words, they must not give in to its perception. This infallibility determines their identity. The identity gives them a false sense that they possess truth. Therefore, they must learn to take their conclusions lightly because this infallibility puts them on a collision course with reality. This will make them not only fallible, but also fragile.

Once strong-willed people put their sense of infallibility in a correct perspective, they will be able to apply the cross to their immovable ideas. This allows God to properly adjust their lines to His truth, allowing them to experience the fullness of His complete work of *redemption*.

As we can see, the ideal or essence of self often determines people's identity. The process creates an identity crisis as it reveals each nature's inability to change personal reality. This fleshly, worldly identity must give way to following Jesus. Following Jesus implies totally becoming identified with Him. Jesus begins to serve as a person's identity. This means He will become their wisdom, righteousness, sanctification, and redemption.[7]

As a person gives way to this new identity in Jesus through self-denial, death to the flesh, and walking in the fullness of Christ, the new man will be resurrected and manifested. Romans 6:4-5 clarifies this,

> Therefore we are buried with him by baptism unto death: that like as Christ was raised from the dead by the glory of the Father, even so we also should walk in newness of life. For if we have been planted together in the likeness of his death, we shall also in the likeness of his resurrection.

---

[7] 1 Corinthians 1:30

The Christian life is contrary to our old man. The old man declares it must live, but the way of the cross states that he must die. The old man wants to slide into heaven without death to its rebellious, contrary ways, but the cross declares it must cease to reign through suffering and death. This suffering and death come through neglect, deprivation, tribulation, and adversity.[8]

The cross of Jesus is a harsh revelation of the old man and what he does with the things of God. He will try to use, defile, or destroy what is of God in our lives. However, life past the cross of Jesus is about the new man being developed in us, and coming forth in power and victory for the glory of God.

The Apostle Paul put it this way in 2 Timothy 2:11-12, "It is a faithful saying: For if we be dead with him, we shall also live with him: If we suffer, we shall also reign with him: if we deny him, he also will deny us." Have you allowed the process of God to bring you to your true identity in Christ? If you haven't, you will eventually be brought to an identity crisis for the sake of your soul.

---

[8] John 16:33; Acts 14:22; 2 Timothy 3:12

10

FINDING OUR
PLACE IN CHRIST

To reach our potential in Christ, we must find our place in Him. After all, our lives are hidden in Him, and we are positionally seated in high places with Him.[1] Sadly, our fallen condition keeps us from realizing this potential.

The selfish disposition makes people vulnerable to fall into various traps. They become established in their arrogance by the world. Their self-sufficiency gives them a false sense of their spiritual condition as they try to create an earthly utopia that is void of God's reign and one that will revolve around them. Their flesh feeds their ego and gives temporary pleasure as a means of enticing them into greater darkness. Eventually, reality reveals their inability to possess a utopia where they reign as god. This creates an identity crisis, causing many to fall into utter despair, resulting in some giving way to anger and aggression.

The percentage of people who come to God out of complete need or desperation is small. Most people ignore, avoid, or deny facing their mortality and their need for God. This need is not only in light of their present state, but their past and future. Each person needs to be cleansed of their past sins, and to be presently

---

[1] Ephesians 2:6; Colossians 3:3

established in righteousness in order to be overcoming in the present, and victorious in the future.

This is what it means to experience wholeness in Christ. To accomplish this, a person needs to recognize their nature. Since each nature has different strengths and weaknesses, God establishes each person in His kingdom according to their strengths and weaknesses.

The Bible points out that man's undisciplined strengths will set him up for a fall. On the other hand, submitted weaknesses become the greatest avenue of strength in God's kingdom.[2] These strengths and weaknesses also determine the type of leadership a person will bring to the kingdom of God. For example, a submissive person may desire the leadership qualities of a strong-willed person, but does not possess the same strengths or weaknesses that will define such leadership. Such a comparison will cause frustration, despair, and condemnation.

The Bible clearly condemns such comparisons. The Apostle Paul said this about this matter in 2 Corinthians 10:12, "For we dare not make ourselves of the number, or compare ourselves with some that commend themselves: but they measuring themselves by themselves, and comparing themselves by themselves, are not wise." It is not wise to compare yourself with those who appear or boast of having a greater measure of spirituality.

Christians are only given one example by which to test or discern themselves, and that is the Person of Jesus Christ. His disposition marks the real quality of leadership. His life marks both the righteous walk and what constitutes an acceptable sacrifice. In order to become this example, He had to become a servant of all. As a result, He was exalted above all.[3]

---

[2] 1 Corinthians 1:29-31; 2 Corinthians 12:9-10
[3] Matthew 11:28-30; Philippians 2:5-11

The secret to finding our place in Christ begins with accepting the way we are made. Our fallen condition always mocks our weaknesses and exalts our strengths above God. But, Jesus gave up His strength and became weak and poor. He took on the disposition of a servant. He instructed us to take on the same disposition. In fact, we are told to learn of Him.[4]

This brings us to what we need to do about personal strengths and weaknesses. As each person realizes strengths must be subdued through submission to the Holy Ghost and weaknesses redefined through the grace of God, they can begin to accept how God has designed them. The main purpose of this design is to reflect the glory of God.

As the character of Christ is defined through a person's weakness, they can begin to discover their leadership and place in His Body. As they present their body as a living sacrifice, the Holy Spirit will discipline and channel personal strength, as well as transform the person's mind. This mind will take on the disposition of Christ, therefore, expressing itself in Christ-like character, attitude, and conduct. It is the reality of Christ in the person that serves as an acceptable fragrance to God, becomes a source of edification to the Body of Christ, and a distinct challenge to the unsaved.[5]

If each person found and took their rightful place in the kingdom of God, the Church would become distinct, powerful, and unstoppable. Sadly, many Christians are lost. They are in an identity crisis that makes them feel as if they are being swallowed up by the demands of life.

Due to the invasion of heresy in the Church, Christians are also falling prey to wolves in sheep's clothing, doctrines of demons, and "another spirit." As a result, some are chasing after other

---

[4] Matthew 11:28; John 13:13-17; 2 Corinthians 8:9
[5] Romans 12:1-2; 2 Corinthians 2:15-16; Philippians 2:5

Christs and believing another gospel. This hodgepodge has caused confusion, defilement of the holy, and has indoctrinated people into super spiritual delusion and great darkness.[6]

This heretical invasion has thwarted the effectiveness of the Church and the unveiling of the image of Christ in His people. The Body of Christ needs to be revived by catching a vision of its real purpose in this world. One of the ways this can be accomplished is by studying the leadership of each nature.

To ensure the spirit behind this information, I asked the Lord to scripturally confirm it. He graciously obliged me by showing me examples of each nature in Scripture. This revelation opened the Word up to me in greater ways. As I studied and meditated on each scriptural example, I could see how God dealt with these individuals according to their nature. It was both exciting and humbling. Interestingly, I found that people often related to the writings and lives of those who had like nature. If you are not sure of your nature, consider the Scriptural examples that you most relate to. These examples might reveal your nature to you.

Submissive Nature

Submission is considered a weakness in most societies. But, godly submission in the kingdom of God is the greatest point of strength and leadership. Jesus made this clear in Matthew 20:27, "And whosoever will be chief among you, let him be your servant."

For submission to become this strength, submissive people must be in submission to Jesus. He must become their focus in order to be established on the immovable Rock of ages. Once they are established on the Rock, they will become pillars in His kingdom. Interestingly, Revelation 3:12 says this, "Him that overcometh will I make a pillar in the temple of my God..." The

---

[6] Matthew 7:15-16; 2 Corinthians 11:1-4; 1 Timothy 4:1

term "pillar" was ascribed to the Apostle John, the beloved, in Galatians 2:9.

The *Apostle John* fits the qualification of a submissive person. His Gospel and epistles reveal someone who presented the truth in an analytical way, by building up a clear presentation as to Jesus' identity. He did this by emphasizing Jesus' teachings in his Gospel.

We see John becoming obnoxious at one point when he wanted to call fire down from heaven upon the Samaritans. But, we also see a sweet, sensitive side when he laid his head on Jesus' chest.[7] In his first epistle, he talked about his personal encounter with Jesus,

> That which was from the beginning, which we have heard, which we have seen with our eyes, which we have looked upon, and our hands have handled, of the Word of life; (For the life was manifested, and we have seen it, and bear witness, and shew unto you that eternal life, which was with the Father, and was manifested unto us;) (1 John 1:1-2).

John's perspective was the Son of God. It established him as a pillar in Jesus' kingdom. He was a strong leader of the new Church. He proved to be bold in his declarations of Him, and ready to offer himself up for the furtherance of His kingdom.

The Apostle John had been surrounded by the reality of Jesus. He was a man compelled by a personal revelation of His Lord, upheld by the reality of His presence, and refined by his identification with Him. However, in Revelation, he would be confronted with a greater revelation of his Lord and Savior that would bring him facedown before Him in fear and dread.

If submissive people fail to have Jesus as their focus, they will give way to fear. We see this happening to *Elijah*. He was a great

---

[7] Luke 9:51-56; John 13:23

prophet of faith. He had stopped the heavens from raining for three years and taken on the prophets of Baal, but when he took his eyes off God and put them on Queen Jezebel, he fled in fear and fell into self-pity.[8]

In spite of his struggles, God met him. Once again, Elijah gained the right perspective that enabled him to finish his course. This is the key behind victory. Submissive people, who have a balanced perspective because of God, can stand and withstand. However, they must be surrounded by His perspective and ways, rather than running in the ruts of their mind to gain understanding.

The means of success for the submissive person can be observed in the life of *Daniel*. He was faced with death more than once. Instead of fainting before the prospects of it, he withdrew into God. God did not fail him and honored him before Gentile leaders. He truly rested on the Rock because he had purposed early in his life and heart to believe Jehovah God and obey Him.[9]

If submissive people have the right eternal perspective, they can be entrusted with much. After all, they are pillars. *Isaiah* had a vision of the Lord in Isaiah 6. He was entrusted with what many consider a miniature Bible within the Word of God. His book reveals the birth, ministry, death, and reign of Christ.

Another submissive person who was entrusted with much was *Mary*, the mother of Jesus. She was sincere in her faith and pure in heart. As a result, God entrusted her with the Messiah.

We also see this in the case of Daniel and the Apostle John. They were given many details about the future or what we know as the end-day events, which are presently unfolding before our very eyes.

---

[8] 1 Kings 17:1; 19:1-15
[9] Daniel 1:8; 3, 6

Are you submissive? Is your focus on self, fear, or Jesus? The answer will determine the extent of your perspective, and how much God will entrust to you.

Stubborn Nature

Stubborn people need proof from God. This is a quality that is often criticized. Surprisingly, God will give the necessary proof as He did to *Gideon* and *Thomas*. Few criticize Gideon for putting out a fleece concerning a matter that had been commanded by God. He not only asked Him to confirm it once, but twice. But, when it comes to Thomas wanting Jesus to prove His existence in the midst of his despair, he is considered "doubting Thomas."[10]

Many stubborn people are misunderstood because they show uncertainty in the midst of challenging times. The problem concerning their uncertainty is that it is much more obvious with them than it is with other natures. The other natures can cover up doubt or uncertainty with wisdom, diplomacy, masks, and games, but stubborn people's struggles are "all out there" for others to see.

Take Peter for example. He is the only one who got out of the boat and walked on water to meet Jesus. However, because he took his eyes off Jesus as the waves loomed in front of him, he is made a constant example of how doubt works. Few ever note that the rest of the disciples stayed in the boat and avoided the fiery test of their faith. This is probably why Peter could effectively address the test of faith in his first epistle.[11] It is easy to be a spectator and critical in these matters, but opinions mean little unless one has been tested. Those who have been tested tend to avoid judging others because of their own personal experiences.

---

[10] Judges 6:36-40; John 20:24-29
[11] Matthew 14:26-33; 1 Peter 1:6-9

Peter is often pointed out for his denial of Jesus. Once again, few note Judas' betrayal of Jesus, while the rest of His disciples abandoned Him altogether. Again, Peter blatantly failed the test, but so did the rest of humanity. Jesus was a test to many types of people during His ordeal to Calvary. If they weren't denying Him, they were beating Him. If they were not betraying Him, they were crucifying Him.

The reason for instability and inconsistency in stubborn people is their emotional makeup. It causes them to be on an emotional roller coaster; therefore, they do not always trust their decisions. They seek proof to confirm what they perceive or have been told.

John the Baptist, in his darkest ordeal, sent his disciples to ask Jesus if He was the Promised One. Jesus did not reprove him for the question. He simply sent the necessary proof back to John to assure him of His identity.[12]

Although stubborn people's emotional instability can cause much grief, it also can serve as an asset. King David was able to express every known emotion in the book of Psalms to reveal the personal, inner struggles that we all face because we live in the flesh. However, his final conclusion was the same: God is real and reigning.

The secret to victory for stubborn people is lining up all their emotions to the cornerstone (examples and words) of Jesus Christ. This will bring the necessary discipline or stability. Emotional stability allows the Holy Ghost to channel their momentum and energy level into bold leadership in the kingdom of God.

We see this boldness in Gideon, David, Nehemiah, John the Baptist, Peter, and even Thomas. The combination of boldness and their sense of fair play can cause these people to become abrasive plumb lines in the Church. Like the prophet, *Jeremiah*,

---

[12] Nehemiah 4:9-18; Jeremiah 4:3; Matthew 11:2-11; John 20:1-18

they will tear up the fallow ground of unregenerate hearts. And, like Nehemiah, they will erect necessary walls of protection, while holding a sword to ensure God's work is done. In the case of *Mary Magdalene*, they will become bold witnesses to His presence and reality in the midst of fear and doubt.[13]

Stubborn people bring a powerful, stable leadership to the kingdom of God. They are able to hold the line of righteousness as they challenge and contend for the souls of others. They will do all they can to line up the living stones of Jesus' Church to the true spiritual Cornerstone of their Lord and Savior, Jesus Christ.[14]

Another aspect that stubborn people must discern and discipline is their emotional sensitivity. These people can be sensitive to the spiritual realm. Like Joseph, Jesus' stepfather, God can communicate with them in dreams.[15] But, if they aren't careful to discern the spirit, they can abuse what some consider man's sixth sense. They will open themselves up to the kingdom of darkness, allowing them to be influenced by demonic powers and doctrines of demons.

Are you stubborn? If so, are you lining up to the Cornerstone, Jesus Christ, so that you are able to bring a bold leadership to God's kingdom?

Self-Assured Nature

Images cause self-assured people to become unpredictable. In fact, if they do not have a vision of the destination or end results of something, they will not finish the course. This is why God must give them distinct vision beyond their images or they will end up taking detours. We see this in the case of Moses. *Moses* was a self-assured person who had the necessary integrity for God to

---

[13] John 11:16
[14] 1 Peter 2:5, 9
[15] Matthew 1:20; 2:19-20

use him. The reason we know this is because of what Hebrews 11:24-25 says, "By faith Moses, when he come to years, refused to be called the son of Pharaoh's daughter; choosing rather to suffer affliction with the people of God, than to enjoy the pleasures of sin for a season."

Moses went through a great boiling process in the wilderness. He had been demoted from the courts of Pharaoh into a base, abominable shepherd. What images he then had fell to the wayside. By the time God met him in the burning bush, Moses' images and identity were pretty well dealt with by his 40-year process.[16]

Moses was now an insecure man who was vulnerable. This vulnerability made him pliable in the Potter's hands. God took his uncertainty and put authority in its place. He took his silent voice and caused it to ring through the corridors of Pharaoh's courts. He replaced his staff with a rod. He exchanged the sheep in the wilderness with the children of Israel. He took an insignificant shepherd and caused His glory to be unveiled before others.[17]

This is the key to victory of the self-assured person. An exchange has to be made in their life. We see such an exchange happening in Moses' life. The courts of Pharaoh were exchanged for the wilderness. The wilderness gave way to Mount Sinai. On Mount Sinai, the vanity of idols and paganism were exposed and replaced by the Law.[18]

We also see an exchange occur in *Jacob's* life. He was a plain man of the tent. He may have appeared to be quiet, but underneath his exterior he had a desire for position and purpose greater than what he possessed in the present world. He understood the character of his brother, Esau. And, at the right

---

[16] Genesis 46:34; Exodus 2:9-15; 3:1-6
[17] Exodus 3:9-16; 4:2-3; 34:28-20
[18] Exodus 20

time his clever qualities came forth. Jacob managed to get his brother to sell his birthright for a bowl of pottage.[19]

Later, he conspired with his mother to possess the blessing. These actions on the part of Jacob put him in a questionable light. But, God knew what was in Jacob's heart. The word "plain" in Genesis 25:27 implies gentle and dear, coupled with perfect, undefiled, and upright.[20] It would take twenty years to bring this disposition forth, but once it was unveiled, it revealed a man of tremendous leadership—a man who ended up blessing the Pharaoh.[21]

An exchange had to be made in Jacob's life. This exchange could not occur until after the process was complete. Esau's murderous attitude towards Jacob forced him to leave his home in search of a new life. The spiritual part of the journey would last two decades. In a sense, it would begin at Bethel when he was on his way to his uncle's place. There, God revealed Himself. Jacob did something of great significance at Bethel in recognition of His encounter with God. He erected a pillar and anointed it with oil. Then, he made a vow to God that if He brought him home, he would make Him God of his life.[22] This means that Jacob was vowing to become a servant of Jehovah God.

Jacob could not develop a servant's disposition on his own. Only God could work this attitude in him. God used Jacob's uncle to accomplish this feat. He would serve as a mirror to Jacob. He was deceptive, shrewd, and sneaky. He concealed certain matters and managed to manipulate Jacob into the position of a servant. In spite of this treatment, Jacob showed integrity and God blessed

---

[19] Genesis 25:27, 29-34
[20] Strong's Exhaustive Concordance of the Bible; #8535
[21] Genesis 27:5-30; 47:7, 10
[22] Genesis 28:11-22

him. In the end, Jacob would serve his uncle for 20 years, while maintaining righteousness.[23]

Possible retribution from Esau awaited Jacob on his return to his homeland. Alone, Jacob faced the possibilities. He had crossed over Jabbok. Jabbok means "emptying". Here he met a heavenly being. He wrestled all night with this being to secure a blessing. This is when an incredible exchange took place. He ceased to be Jacob, "the supplanter," and became Israel, "the prince that prevails with God." Jacob was no longer Jacob, but a man of God, a servant of God who had overcome.[24]

The disposition of a servant brings us back to Jacob's action in Bethel. He erected a pillar and anointed it. Once self-assured people are emptied of their prideful ways, Jesus, the Rock of Ages, can be erected in their lives. At this point, they can become the anointed servants of God. Interestingly enough, God refers to godly self-assured people as His servants.[25] We see this in the case of Job.

Job had a righteous life that could clearly be seen by others. His life before God caused God to point him out to Satan as an example. Satan rose up to wipe that perfect, undefiled image out by testing Job in areas that would cause the best devotee of God to fall into disbelief and anger. Satan touched Job's possessions, his family, and then his health.[26]

Job encountered questions, confusion, and accusations throughout his trial, but He never cursed God. As he struggled with beliefs that were proving limited and inept, he held on to the character of God, knowing that one day he would be resurrected into His unending and glorious presence. He maintained that he was being refined as gold through this process, and declared that

---

[23] Genesis 30:33; 31:1-18
[24] Genesis 32:22-32
[25] Job 1:8, see also Exodus 14:31
[26] Job 1 & 2

even if God should slay him, he would choose to trust Him. Job was indeed righteous **before** God, but the process would make him righteous **in** and **because** of God when he came out with a greater sense of God in His holiness and majesty.[27]

Job did all the right things, but he failed to remember that the source of all righteousness is found in God. God had given Job the heart, the means, and the vision to be righteous before Him. Job could never take credit for the righteousness that was being manifested in his life through disposition and actions. At the end of his ordeal, he could only declare, "I have heard of thee by the hearing of the ear: but now mine eye seeth thee. Wherefore I abhor myself, and repent in dust and ashes" (Job 42:5-6).

When self-assured people's fierceness is channeled in a right way, they will wrestle in prayer and ensure the promises of God are upheld in integrity. For example, Moses interceded on behalf of Israel when God threatened to destroy Israel after the people refused to enter the Promised Land. Sarah, the wife of Abraham, protected Isaac's inheritance. She knew Isaac was not to share his inheritance with Ishmael. She demanded that Abraham send Ishmael and his mother away. God commanded Abraham to obey her.[28]

Fierceness that is properly channeled will enable the self-assured person to make the commitment to become the strong leader in God's kingdom. This will allow the Holy Ghost to transform their perception and agendas by aligning their standards to the disposition and example of Jesus. This will cause the self-assured person to become singular in heart and vision.

Pride remains a big issue for these people. Their images along with indecisiveness and fear of incompetence can place them at precarious places of judgment. Moses failed to circumcise his

---

[27] Job 13:15; 91:25-27; 23:10
[28] Genesis 21:1-13; Numbers 14

sons and almost lost his life. At the end of the journey through the wilderness, he gave way to his anger, allowing self-sufficiency to arise. In this state, He disobeyed God concerning the rock in the wilderness, and never entered the Promised Land. As he was instructing the people of Israel about the Law of God, he blamed them for his judgment. However, God set the record straight when He sent Moses up to Mount Nebo to die. He clearly stipulated that the judgment was the result of what Moses did.[29]

We can also clearly see the results of pride in King Saul and King Ahab's lives. As you study Saul's life, you see where he had no inclination to obey God as he walked according to the flesh. He showed worldly remorse when called to accountability by the prophet Samuel, but he never really repented or changed his way of being. Eventually, the Spirit of God departed from him.[30]

Ahab was idolatrous and greedy. He was moody when he didn't get his way. But, Ahab walked lightly before God when confronted by Elijah over the murder of Naboth.[31] However, this only lasted for a season, and Ahab was back to his old ways.

These people display self-pity when called to accountability. Self-pity is nothing more than worldly sorrow. This can be observed in the lives of Cain and Judas Iscariot. Cain killed his brother, but felt sorry for himself when God called him to accountability. Judas Iscariot regretted that he betrayed an innocent man (the Son of God), and tried to give the money back to the priests. When the Chief Priest refused to free him of his guilt, he hung himself.[32]

Self-assured people can be assured of one thing, God will call them to accountability whether in this present world or at the last judgment. They need to test themselves according to fruits rather

---

[29] Exodus 4:24-26; Deuteronomy 3:23-26; 32:49-51
[30] 1 Samuel 15; 16:14
[31] 1 Kings 21:29
[32] Genesis 4:8-15; Matthew 27:3-10

than images. Repentance must get past the images and emotional level down into the heart where integrity must prevail. They must wrestle before God to become empty, in order to become a servant in disposition.

Once self-assured people get past the façades, God can meet them in truth. At this point, they will receive a vision that will enable them to finish the course. After all, Jacob witnessed the ladder between heaven and earth, Moses knew God's presence and saw His glory, and God revealed Himself to Job through His creation. These men possessed heavenly visions beyond this world. And, what powerful leaders and examples they became in the kingdom of God.

Strong-Willed Nature

Strong-willed people bring decisive leadership to the kingdom of God by bringing clarity to the things of God. For example, the Apostle Paul brought decisive instructions to the new Church in his many epistles. He instructed them in the ways of righteousness.

The key behind the validity of a strong-willed person's leadership is determined by who they are serving. These people will reflect the very attitudes and attributes of those they follow. This is brought out in the leaderships of Deborah, the judge and prophetess, and Queen Jezebel. Deborah displayed the righteousness and the victory of Jehovah God, while Jezebel reflected the demonic influences, wickedness, and practices of her idolatrous, pagan god, Baal.[33]

God's dealing with these people is distinct as well. The Apostle Paul started out persecuting Christians. On the road to Damascus, he encountered the real Jesus. He was not only brought down to his knees, but he lost his eyesight. This proud Pharisee had to be

---

[33] Judges 4 & 5; 1 Kings 16:28-33; 19:1-3; 21:17-25

led by the hand. Talk about an extreme process! But, this incident turned Paul around to walk in the light of Jesus.[34]

The prophet Jonah and King Nebuchadnezzar are other examples of strong-willed people doing an about-face because of extreme processes. God prepared a fish for rebellious Jonah. Needless to say, the fish changed Jonah's mind and direction, bringing him into obedience to God.[35]

After being warned by Daniel about taking credit for his kingdom, Nebuchadnezzar was driven into a field where he ate grass as an ox for seven years.[36] At the end of seven years, his senses returned. This was his humble declaration, "Now I Nebuchadnezzar praise and extol and honor the King of heaven, all whose works are truth, and his ways judgment: and those that walk in pride he is able to abase" (Daniel 4:37).

Strong-willed people, who are being ruled by God, prove to be trustworthy. We see this in the life of Jacob's son Joseph. Betrayed and sold into slavery by his brothers, he maintained his uprightness. Even after being falsely accused and imprisoned, he upheld his integrity. Through his ordeal, God gave him favor until he was exalted as a powerful leader in Egypt.[37]

In both the lives of the Apostle Paul and King Nebuchadnezzar, we read about the rock. In Nebuchadnezzar, the rock or stone came as judgment on all earthly kingdoms, giving way to an eternal King and His kingdom. Jesus talked about being the Stone that man would trip over and be broken, producing eternal life, or else be utterly crushed by Him in judgment. [38]

---

[34] Acts 9
[35] Jonah 1-3:1
[36] Daniel 4
[37] Genesis 37:8-36; 39-41
[38] Daniel 2:44-45; Matthew 21:44; 1 Corinthians 10:4-10

The Rock in Paul's case was the one found in the wilderness that was struck by Moses. It miraculously gave water to the thirsty people. This incident pointed to Jesus who was struck by man in the wilderness of suffering and death. Out of Him, came rivers of Living Water for all who will come to Him.[39]

The reality of this Rock is that it will either bring life to the thirsty or judgment to those who discard and abuse its provision. Such judgment points to separation.

The cross of Jesus brings a separation and decisiveness to the world. A person will not leave this world untouched by this Rock. It will either break them, bringing them unto repentance, or in judgment, while grinding them into powder. Godly strong-willed people have the ability to cause this decisive separation in the kingdom of God. They will reflect God's attributes as well as cut away at the heart of personal justification and compromise.

These people's ability to bring powerful, decisive leadership is clearly exposed by Joseph, Jonah, and the Apostle Paul. Joseph was used to save his family, Jonah's preaching saved a whole city, and the Apostle Paul opened up the kingdom of God to the entire Gentile world.

Strong-willed people's potential can only be discovered when they give up their need to rule their worlds. This means they must come into obedience under the rule of God.

Are you strong-willed and under the control of God's Spirit, or are you subjected to other masters? This will determine whether you reach your potential in God's kingdom or waste your life, causing you to reap the consequences for eternity.

---

[39] John 7:37-39

11

THE REFLECTION
OF CHRIST

My co-laborer, Jeannette, was at first suspicious about the spiritual validity of the nature information. She was leery of self-help programs or information that found its roots in psychology or the four temperaments. In spite of her doubts about the information, she remained a true friend because she knew we had agreement in almost every other scriptural matter.

She patiently listened to my ramblings about the nature information while silently wondering if I was operating with a mixed spirit. In other words, whether at different times I was operating with the right spirit while occasionally coming under a wrong spirit due to fleshly and worldly agreements. However, God eventually put the nature information to a test where she was concerned.

We were in a precarious situation where Jeannette had to consult with a pastor about another minister. To ensure effective results, I told her how to approach this pastor based on his nature. She followed my instructions. To her surprise, it was an effective meeting. She began to earnestly listen to me, as well as ask questions. A new world opened up to her as she began to understand her relationships with others.

It was not long before Jeannette became an enthusiastic supporter of the Hidden Manna information. As a result, God began to give her insight into the natures. In fact, she was given one of the most humbling and powerful revelations of Jesus Christ.

It is not my cause to promote the Hidden Manna information. It is simply a tool that has helped others, as well as me, to effectively minister to people. My main heart is Jesus Christ and Him crucified. Jesus is the only One who can save. He heals the broken hearted and sets the captive free.[1]

Therefore, my main spiritual search is not to understand human nature, but to find Jesus in His Word and creation, as well as to witness His attitude and life in His Body. Because of this desire, He has never failed me as far as substantiating and revealing Himself in Scripture, as well as in the nature information. In this case, He revealed to Jeannette how these different natures put together in the Body serve as a powerful revelation of Him. And, through a series of situations, He revealed the name or reference to the nature information: *Hidden Manna.*

I was reminded of the manna of old. It came from heaven. The Israelites perceived it as a foreign substance, but God told them to gather it and partake of it. It not only gave them life, but also proved to be satisfying. Jesus confirmed that this manna pointed to Him as the Bread from heaven.[2]

There are so many aspects about Jesus that are hidden.[3] The Holy Ghost unveils each revelation about Him and bids His followers to partake of it. Each nugget brings greater meaning to our spiritual walk and life, producing satisfaction and contentment in the soul.

There are also treasures or nuggets of Jesus that are veiled in humanity. Only through the work of the Holy Ghost can these treasures be uncovered. As the Lord began to reveal this gold mine hidden in humanity, I was reminded of Revelation 2:17,

---

[1] Luke 4:18; 1 Corinthians 2:2
[2] Exodus 16:4, 11-36; John 6:32-40
[3] Colossians 1:26-27, 2:2-3

He that hath an ear, let him hear what the Spirit saith unto the churches; To him that overcometh will I give to eat of the hidden manna, and will give him a white stone, and in the stone a new name written, which no man knoweth saving he that receiveth it.

Jesus' followers must overcome to truly eat of the manna, and to receive the stone that has a new name written on it. The manifestation of this overcoming will be the unveiling of Jesus in power and glory in the believer's life.

Jeannette received this information when we were about to minister in an obscure place in Arizona. Immediately, we implemented it into the Hidden Manna Seminar. This revelation has overwhelmed, humbled, and brought sobriety to those who have heard it. Those who hear the Hidden Manna information begin considering what it means for them to get beyond acceptable religious boundaries and scale the heights that God has divinely ordained for each nature in the Body of Christ.

Keep in mind that in the beginning, God made man in the image, likeness, and resemblance of Himself. Therefore, man was to reflect the glory of God. When Adam disobeyed God, he fell into darkness. Needless to say, the ability to reflect God's glory was darkened and marred. As Romans 3:23 says, "For all have sinned, and come short of the glory of God."

Jesus Christ put off His former glory or His sovereignty as deity and took on the shape of man. He reflected the Father and served as a mirror to mankind. Through His redemption on the cross, He established the way in which people can once again serve as a reflection of God. Granted, the veil must be taken off of a person's heart and mind, but Jesus is able to accomplish this. This allows freedom for the Spirit of God to work Jesus' life in His followers, thereby, reflecting Him in and to the world.[4]

---

[4] Philippians 2:6-8; 2 Corinthians 3:13-18; 4:3-5

Christians who give way to the Holy Ghost's work will reflect Christ. Depending on their nature, they will reflect various aspects of Jesus in different ways. These different reflections do not contradict one another, but simply add dimension to His character and reality.

The Apostle Paul tells us that God takes each believer and places them individually in the Body of Christ.[5] If each believer allows the reality of Christ to shine forth, what kind of reflection or image would emerge in Jesus' incredible Body? You would have a powerful, complete picture of Jesus Christ.

This was brought to light by two Scriptures: Ezekiel 1:10 and Revelation 4:7. These Scripture verses are in regards to the four beasts: the lion, the ox or calf, the man, and the eagle. These four beasts represent the universal reign of Christ over all of creation, therefore encompassing all four directions of the earth.

There are also four Gospels. As you study these four Gospels, you realize that each of these four symbols or aspects of Jesus' reign is represented in the Gospels. As you consider the four creatures in light of the four natures, once again, you can see these four representations in the natures. Each of these creatures give much needed insight into what each nature must overcome to personally and collectively become the reflection of Christ in this lost world.

As a person associates the creature to the right nature, they will unveil the Gospel that was written for their particular nature. As each line connects with the dots, a powerful revelation of Jesus is uncovered along with the potential of the Body of Christ in this world. This potential is immeasurable. However, for the Body to reach its heights in God, each nature must overcome that which would mar Jesus' reflection in their life, and allow God to fit them into the Body.

---

[5] 1 Corinthians 12:18

Let us now consider this incredible revelation.

Strong-Willed Nature

The first Gospel is Matthew. It was written to the Jews to prove that Jesus was and is their Promised King and Messiah. It revealed that He is from the tribe of Judah and of the lineage of King David. As the oldest son of Joseph, Jesus was in line to the throne of David. This lineage was of the uttermost importance, because a king was promised from the lineage of David. This king would establish David's throne forever.[6]

Jacob also made reference to this leader when he prophesied over Judah,

> Judah is a lion's whelp: from the prey, my son, thou art gone up: he stooped down, he couched as a lion, and as an old lion; who shall rouse him up? The scepter shall not depart from Judah, nor a lawgiver from between his feet, until Shiloh come; and unto him shall the gathering of the people be (Genesis 49:9-10).

This prophecy is pointing to Jesus, the Lion of the tribe of Judah. This reveals the symbol associated with the Gospel of Matthew, the *lion*.

Matthew not only establishes Jesus' identity as King and the lion prophesied in *Genesis* by recording His lineage, but he also confirms His identity by pointing out how seven prophecies were fulfilled concerning His coming in the first four chapters of this Gospel.[7] As one considers the facts, decisiveness, and emphasis of the Gospel of Matthew, they can see how it is written to the strong-willed person.

The lion is also the symbol that strong-willed people gladly embrace. He is considered the king of all the wild beasts. He is

---

[6] 2 Samuel 7:12-16
[7] Matthew 1:23; 2:5-6, 14-15, 17-18, 22-23; 3:3; 4:14-16

powerful, and can intimidate or bring fear to the hearts of almost all who cross his path. Strong-willed people can prove to be both powerful and intimidating leaders. They have the potential of ruling much, but can easily display improper leadership when not being ruled by the King of kings and Lord of lords.

This brings us to the dangers of the lion. Strong-willed people may like the concept of being a lion, but they must keep in mind how dangerous this beast can be. It preys on other creatures in order to rule. It can be indifferent, ruthless, and cruel regardless of the circumstances. This can also be true for strong-willed people who are not under the control of the Holy Ghost. They prey on other people in order to control their worlds. They can be indifferent to needs, ruthless in pursuits, and cruel in their handling of matters. Such attributes are contrary to the disposition of Jesus.

There are four distinct attributes associated with a powerful reign: *authority*, *royalty*, *strength*, and *power*. All of these attributes are attractive to a strong-willed person, but the secret is that there must be balance that comes in the form of godly boundaries.

Scripture reveals this balance by always presenting the lion in conjunction with the lamb. We see this in the case of Jesus. In Revelation 5:5-6, the Apostle John is ready to behold the Lion of Judah, but what he beholds is the Lamb that was slain before the foundation of the world. Interestingly, the Lion of Judah is always depicted in conjunction with the meek, sacrificial Lamb. This means that proper balance can only come to the strong-willed person when they take on the disposition of the lamb.

How does one with the capabilities of a lion develop a disposition of the lamb? And, how can they display the attributes of leadership that will benefit the Church and bring glory to God? For example, it is easy for a lion to possess natural authority, but how does a lamb display that authority?

Scripture tells us through gentleness. "Thou hast also given me the shield of thy salvation: and thy right hand hath holden me

117

up, and thy gentleness hath made me great" (Psalm 18:35). The word great means "to increase or be in authority."[8] This shows that godly authority is established through the attitude of gentleness and not intimidation or aggression.

Royalty means "to rule sovereignly, kingly, and a foundation of power or dominion."[9] How does one gain the position of royalty in God's kingdom? This position can only be obtained through humility. Matthew 5:3 says, "Blessed are the poor in spirit; for theirs is the kingdom of heaven." The word "poor" in this text means "beggar" or "cringing pauper."[10] Such an attitude points to one who is in need and is vulnerable. Such a concept is far from the strong-willed person who insists on putting confidence in personal strength, rather than regress and trust God. But, to those with the disposition of a lamb, meekness is a natural response.

Strength is the third trait. It implies to fasten upon, seize, conquer, withstand, might, and prevail.[11] In what way does a strong-willed person display strength? Matthew 5:5 tells us through the disposition of meekness, "Blessed are the meek: for they shall inherit the earth." Meekness implies that a person's strength is under the control of the Holy Spirit. Therefore, it will never be abusive and destructive.

Strong-willed people want to rule their worlds and often display an *unruly spirit* that opposes God's authority. Until they become properly ruled, they become the ones who will eventually be conquered by their own fear. This fear will cause them to pull their world down around them. In other words, their own strength will end up destroying them. It is only by taking on the disposition of the lamb that their strength can be used in a proper way to inherit

---

[8] Strong's Exhaustive Concordance #7235
[9] Ibid #4467
[10] Ibid #4434
[11] Ibid #202, 3581

all that God has for them. This disposition means total surrender to the real King of kings.

The final attribute of a king and a lion is power. Strong-willed people can only display power in a proper way when they are under right authority. They must remember where real strength and power come from, "…Not by might, nor by power, but by my spirit, saith the LORD of hosts" (Zechariah 4:6).

When strong-willed people are unruly, they will draw their own lines and rules. These lines may run parallel to God, but they will not be within the righteous boundaries or ways of God. Interestingly, one of the definitions of rule is "to mark with parallel lines."[12] These people will always have lines or boundaries, but God must be the One who establishes the location of these lines.

Strong-willed people must give up the need to control, and submit to the gentle guidance of the Spirit. The Apostle Paul brought this out as he instructed believers to follow him as he followed Christ. Paul had lost his strength as a lion on the road to Damascus, but found real life and authority in Jesus.[13] He became a meek, obedient lamb that willingly followed the Lion of Judah. In the end, he was able to make this declaration:

> For I am now ready to be offered, and the time of my departure is at hand. I have fought a good fight, I have finished my course, I have kept the faith: Henceforth there is laid up for me a crown of righteousness which the Lord, the righteous judge, shall give me at that day:... (2 Timothy 4:6-8).

---

[12] Webster's New Collegiate Dictionary
[13] Acts 9; 1 Corinthians 11:1

Stubborn Nature

Mark, the second Gospel depicts Jesus as the burden bearer or the sacrificial ox that carried our sins to the cross. It is a fast moving Gospel, and is full of proof as it speaks of the many miracles of Jesus. Many believed the stubborn Peter dictated this Gospel to Mark. These aspects of this Gospel all point to the stubborn person. Therefore, the ox or calf serves as the symbol for this nature.

Stubborn people have a problem with the ox representing their nature. It often causes sobriety rather than joy. They initially see themselves as free spirited, ready to embrace and experience the world in glorious ecstasy, rather than being tied to a cart or plow. They feel more like a wild stallion that refuses to be caught or tamed, instead of an ox ready to be led to the altar of sacrifice. Feeling like a wild horse is nothing more than a fantasy, but these people can stubbornly hold onto it.

The reality behind these people is clearly revealed when they are challenged, abused, hurt, and wounded. They don't run like a horse to escape the situation, but will charge like a raging bull. As a result, they often leave a path of confusion and destruction behind them.

Because stubborn people enjoy their fantasy about being a wild horse, they often balk at the concept of being nothing more than a cow, prepared to be offered up as a sacrifice. Their response is normally in compliance with their *undisciplined spirit*. It also explains what God wants to do with stubborn people by using the contrast of the ox. The ox is the king of all the tame beasts; therefore, God truly wants to discipline the emotions, purpose, and walk of this individual to bring forth their potential in the kingdom of God.

Two things must occur for stubborn people to experience godly discipline: 1) They must become yoked with Christ, and 2) they must be willing to be sacrificed. The reason for this is because stubborn people have the ability to plow up the fallow ground of people's hearts with their honesty and bluntness. Even when stubborn people try to be diplomatic about the truths of God, they still manage to cause friction. In turn, those offended will turn around and sacrifice them. Unless stubborn people realize that this sacrifice is an affront against truth and righteousness, they will take it personally and interpret it as rejection.

This brings us to the importance of the yoke. Stubborn people must be yoked with Jesus to keep matters in perspective. If these people remain under the yoke of Jesus, they will be able to confidently hide in Him regardless of the attitudes, expressions, and actions of others.

Jesus' yoke will also bring stubborn people to the altar of the cross. This yoke points to the disciplined walk of self-denial and death. As stubborn people submit to the yoke, they begin to take on the disposition of Jesus. As they give way to the work and the leading of the yoke, they become identified with Him in His sufferings. This identification will make them into leaders who have been consecrated to reign with Him.[14] It is in this disciplined walk that Jesus deals with their selfishness.

Once selfishness is dealt with, stubborn people can become the acceptable sacrifice. They will be ready to be offered up at all times for the sake of Christ. Hebrews 12:2 reveals Jesus' attitude about the sacrifice He made on our behalf, "Looking unto Jesus the author and finisher of our faith; who for the joy that was set before him endured the cross, despising the shame, and is set down at the right hand of the throne of God." He endured the cross, joyfully knowing the outcome. Likewise, stubborn people can joyfully endure the cross, knowing that victory awaits them.

---

[14] 2 Timothy 2:12

There is also another significance to Hebrews 12:2. Scholars believe that this Scripture verse refers back to the sacrifices that were offered up by the Levitical priests. The priests were required to examine each part of the sacrifice. As one considers each area in light of stubborn people becoming yoked with Christ and walking out the sacrificial life as a living sacrifice, they can begin to understand those areas that must be disciplined.

The first area that was examined on the sacrifice was the *head*. Head represents the intelligence and thoughts. Everyone has to recognize the need to discipline the focus of their intelligence in order to control their thoughts. Since stubborn people have an emotional momentum that leads them into a world of fantasy, they must avoid the tendency to go with their feelings. The key to this discipline is found in Philippians 2:5, "Let this mind be in you, which was also in Christ Jesus." The word "let" implies discipline. This discipline occurs when one gives way to the work of God.

The second part that needed to be examined was the *fat*. The fat represents the general vigor or excellence of the sacrifice. To the Christian, the fat represents what they are offering. Much of what the American Church offers is unacceptable because it is not marked with a price tag. In other words, the sacrifice never comes out of one's need, but one's leftovers or abundance. Such a sacrifice represents second best, which is marred, blemished, and unacceptable to God. This blemish is a product of selfishness. It is marked by a lack of devotion to God and marred by the absence of genuine sacrifice.

King David made an important point to Araunah in regard to obtaining the land to offer a sacrifice to stay judgment upon Jerusalem. Araunah had offered David the land free of charge. David's reply was, "Nay; but I will surely buy it of thee at a price: neither will I offer burnt offerings unto the LORD my God of that which doth cost me nothing" (2 Samuel 24:24).

If a stubborn person gets past selfishness, they will be liberal in their sacrifice. Such sacrifice is acceptable and pleasing to God.[15] Scriptures make reference to this liberality. Proverbs 11:25 tells us that the soul shall be made fat, and he that waters shall be watered. Psalm 92:12-15 implies that the righteous shall be fat and flourishing. Fat in these Scriptures means "to anoint, to satisfy, to be rich, and fertile."[16]

Obviously, if a person brings the best to God, He will anoint it for His use. God will then satisfy such individuals with a greater reality of Himself. His manifested life in the person will cause them to be rich with heavenly treasures, and will cause them to be productive for His kingdom.

The third area the priests examined of the sacrifice was the inward parts. This represented the motives and affections. Colossians 3:2 instructs believers to set their affections on things above and not on things on the earth. If the affections of the stubborn person are directed at the right source, the motivation will eventually come into line with Jesus' heart. At the core of His heart is sacrificial love that was expressed in obedience. This love is devoid of self and alive with steadfastness to carry out God's will as a servant and as a burden bearer.

Finally, the priest examined the legs of the sacrificial animal. The legs represent the *walk*. The Apostle John stipulates how one must walk in 1 John 2:6, "He that saith he abideth in him ought himself also so to walk, even as he walked." This is in relationship to Jesus.

Jesus serves as our example. He left us with two examples: that of servitude and suffering.[17] As a servant, He submitted to the will of the Father. As a sacrifice, he became obedient to the suffering of the cross.

---

[15] Hebrews 13:15-16
[16] Strong's Exhaustive Concordance #1879
[17] John 13:14-16

Jesus' walk led Him up the narrow path to Calvary. The Christian walk leads up the same narrow path in servitude and sacrifice. This brings His followers in line with God's way, and in obedience to His will. Therefore, stubborn people must consider if they are under the yoke of Christ to ensure the reality of His sacrifice. These two points of discipline will actually discipline their walk.

Interestingly, the strength of the ox must be disciplined before it can become the king of the tame beasts. Discipline helps this animal reach its leadership potential in God's scheme of things. Otherwise, this beast is subject to those things which will prey upon its weakness, leaving it unprotected.

Jeannette discovered some interesting facts about the ox. Discipline for the ox must start at day one. If a calf is not handled immediately, it will become a roaming beast that will become impossible to discipline. Oxen will not respond to brutal treatment, but can be trained to respond to vocal commands. Oxen do not need elaborate harnesses and bits like horses. Just a simple yoke can guide their steps and ensure effective work.

The Apostle Peter understood the necessity of this yoke. Jesus told him that one day he would be guided where he had no intention to walk.[18] This was to stipulate his sacrificial death. This assured him that no matter how his emotions fluctuated, he would stay the course and become an acceptable sacrifice to God.

If you are stubborn, are you yoked with Jesus? Are you becoming an acceptable sacrifice that is ready and willing to be offered up for the glory of God?

Self-Assured Nature

The third Gospel of *Luke* is where Jesus is portrayed as the Son of man. His lineage went back to both Adam and God. This brings

---

[18] John 21:18

us to the conclusion that the third Gospel is associated with the man in the four beasts. Jesus as man reflected what the normal, perfect man would have become before sin entered the picture. But, He also served as the visible image of God.[19] The words "reflection" and "image" immediately identify the nature that is represented by this particular Gospel and symbol—the self-assured nature.

Man is the crowning glory of creation. Adam was formed to reflect the glory of God in the midst of creation. When he sinned against God, that image was marred, preventing him from reaching his ultimate potential.

Jesus was fashioned as a man; therefore, He was capable of representing the perfect man in creation. Hebrews 7:26 gives us insight into this perfection, "For such an high priest became us, who is holy, harmless, undefiled, separate form sinners, and made higher than the heavens."

This Scripture verse says four things about what constitutes perfection. A person must be holy. This means they must be upright in disposition and conduct. A person must be harmless, or in other words, innocent, simple or unsuspecting in attitude. They must be undefiled or unsoiled by the world. And, they must be separate from sinners in every area of his or her heart, mind, and lifestyle.

Many people can respect the qualities of the perfect man, but maintain that Jesus could only fit such qualifications. Once again, the Word refutes this argument. There is a man that fits this criterion. His name is Job. Job 1:1 gives this insight into his character, "There was a man in the land of Uz, whose name was Job; and that man was perfect and upright, and one that feared God, and eschewed evil."

---

[19] Luke 3:23-38; John 14:7; Colossians 2:9; 1 Corinthians 15:44-49

Job was considered perfect in his generation. This means he was complete, pious, gentle, dear, and undefiled.[20] He was complete in his devotion, pious in his actions, gentle in attitude, dear or precious to God, and unspoiled by the world.

Job was also upright. This means Job was straight, direct, fit, and seem good.[21] Being upright pointed to his walk. He stood upright before God. He was consistent in his life, steadfast in his course, fit for God's use, and morally upright.

Job feared God. Such fear serves as a point of discipline. At the heart of this fear is humility. It causes people to show discretion in their walk. This discretion is a manifestation of godly wisdom. Psalm 111:10 states, "The fear of the LORD is the beginning of wisdom..."

Finally, Job hated evil. To hate evil means to hold the line of righteousness regardless of what it personally costs. Job would not turn to the left or right, but maintained his life, testimony, and walk before God.

Job's perfection expressed his inward disposition. His perfection pointed to how complete his commitment was to God for there was no deviation in his faith. His uprightness once again pointed to a walk that was straight in conduct and practices. Fear of the LORD represented his perception, and hatred of evil speaks of his attitude towards the holy and the unholy. As a result, Job represented a sanctified man who stood perfect before God.

Job stood perfect before God, but he was not a perfect, sinless man. Jesus is the only One who remained sinless. This sinless man, who is considered the second man or second Adam, went to the depths of the grave and death so that man could reach perfection in Him.

---

[20] Strong's Exhaustive Concordance #8535
[21] Ibid #3474

Let's now consider the first and the second Adam. The first Adam was created in the image of God. He had the ability to reflect the glory of God. The fact that he had the capacity to reflect the image of God implies that he was self-assured by nature. Do the rest of his actions confirm his nature? He had a choice between the tree of life and the tree of knowledge of good and evil. The fact that he failed to choose either one of them up front points to indecisiveness. When confronted over his sin, he blamed both Eve and God. In his bid to claim independence from God's reign, he exchanged his ability to reflect the glory of God with an angel of light image. This image can be religious, but remain independent and *unyielding* towards God's reign. Instead of operating in a right spirit, it hides behind a beguiling spirit that will strive to seduce people into worshipping an image instead of God. Rather than being upright, this image is crafty and shrewd due to its self-centeredness. Instead of being steadfast, it is unpredictable, causing confusion. Rather than being faithful to God, it becomes treacherous in its motives and dealings. This religious image gives the impression of perfection, but lacks the inward work of sanctification. It becomes a sick substitute for what is real and acceptable.

In the future, the world will have to contend with such an image. This person will come across as the Promised Messiah, but behind the façade is someone who is crafty, beguiling, and seductive. His whole goal is to get the world to bow down and worship him. We know him as the antichrist.

This brings us to the second Adam, Jesus. Jesus was fully God and fully Man. You can only have one nature; therefore, as the Man, what is Jesus' nature? Is it the same as the first Adam? Jesus gives us insight into this subject when He told Philip that He was the physical representative of the Father. He actually reflected the Father's heart, mind, and will. We, therefore, can only conclude that Jesus Christ is self-assured by nature.

If you noticed, the spiritual examples given in the previous chapter for the self-assured were all from the Old Testament. When Jesus' nature as man was being unveiled as being self-assured, I realized why I was not given any New Testament examples. In the Old Testament, Job proved that one can stand perfect before God, but Jesus in His humanity revealed how one becomes perfect in God. He revealed the complete work of sanctification that is done inwardly by the Holy Spirit.

The desire of self-assured people is to be perfect. This is why they develop different images, but Jesus' example reveals that they only have to have one image—His. All these people have to do is yield to the work of the Spirit and He will change their disposition from an *unyielding*, independent spirit to that of a servant. Keep in mind that Jesus emptied Himself of His glory and took on the disposition of a servant and was fashioned as a man.[22] To be a perfect person, a self-assured person must get rid of their vainglory displayed in images and allow the Holy Spirit to develop the disposition of Jesus. Once His disposition is erected, they will reflect the perfect Man in this world.

The ability to reflect this perfect Man gives a small insight into this nature's potential. The potential to reflect the unhindered glory of Jesus in this dark world is incredible. Is it any wonder that Satan tried to wipe this image out by coming against Job? And, consider how he came against Jesus. Satan will do anything to wipe the true image out of the world whether he has to drown it out, counterfeit it, or destroy it.

Luke is a Gospel of contrasts. This nature needs contrast. For example, there is the contrast between the first Adam and the second Adam. The first Adam provides the harsh reality and hypocrisy that is evident with any façade, while the second Adam, Jesus, brings a contrast by defining the disposition and attitude

---

[22] Philippians 2:6-8

that promotes godliness and perfection and reflects the glory of heaven.

These contrasts are brought out in Luke's many parables. One can discover incredible insights in studying these stories. They bring out the clear differences that convey instruction concerning acceptable attitudes and godliness.

Are you self-assured? Are you reflecting the image of Jesus? If you don't reflect His image, consider if you have applied the cross to your images and yielded to the work of the Holy Spirit. In order to do this, you must exchange your logic with integrity and offer up all of your vainglory.

Submissive Nature

Perspective is everything to a submissive nature. The person with this nature will either prove to be a turkey that is earthbound or an eagle that soars in the heavenly realms. This brings us to the fourth Gospel, John.

The Gospel of John is written to unveil Jesus as the Son of God. In order to do this, it opens by giving a heavenly perspective, "In the beginning was the Word, and the Word was with God, and the Word was God" (John 1:1). Not only is Jesus revealed in His pre-incarnate state in the first chapter, but He is also declared the life and light of man, as well as abounding in grace and truth. This incredible revelation continues as Jesus' teachings are intertwined in this Gospel. We are given insight into His wisdom, and we can only conclude that He is wisdom Personified. We witness His first known miracle of turning water into wine. It is in this Gospel that we find Jesus' last teachings and prayer the night He was betrayed. It reveals His heart as He leaves His disciples with indelible examples, as well as simple, life-changing truths and instructions.

The eagle is the only beast that could symbolize this heavenly and incredible perspective. The eagle is the king of all birds. This may seem insignificant in light of the other three creatures unless you realize some simple facts. Lions may claim to be the king of all the wild beasts, but they cannot reach the heights of an eagle. The ox can speak of its strength and sacrifice, but an eagle manifests the ability to find sources of power and strength that will enable it to reach down from great heights to glean from the depths of streams, rivers, and valleys. Man has the ability to reflect the glory of God, but an eagle has the ability to witness God's unhindered glory from the heights of the air currents of His Spirit.

When Jeannette considered how the fearful submissive person had the potential to be an eagle, she marveled. How could people who run in mental ruts reach such heights in God? The answer rests with their ability to seek out such heights and embrace an eternal perspective. For example, Isaiah's perspective was God's glory as His train filled the temple. The Apostle John had a revelation of Jesus in His power and glory. These different perspectives brought these two men low in humility so that they could be brought higher in their understanding and life before God.[23]

Submissive people can be *unmanageable* unless they have an eternal perspective. They become bogged down in their mind. This causes great frustration and depression. As they look to their mind, unresolved matters begin to take over as they ignore, file away, and try to figure out how to resolve issues. Eventually, their conceit and understanding are brought low in the form of failure. It is at this point that they can look up to embrace God's wisdom.

Submissive people's fear also brings them to the end of self so they can be lifted up. Their need to understand brings them to grave depression. This causes desperation. At this point, many

---

[23] Isaiah 6; Revelation 1

submissive people will look up, allowing their understanding to be channeled upward towards the eternal rather than the earthly.

This much needed heavenly perspective for the submissive person is brought out by using the example of the eagle. Job 39:27-29 says, "Does the eagle mount up at your command, and make her nest on high? She dwells and abides on the rock, upon the crag of the rock, and the strong place. From there she sees the prey, and her eyes behold afar off." Jesus must be the Rock and strong place for the submissive person. If they lift up Christ, He will lift them up, giving His perspective.

Once eagles begin to soar on the wind, they can go higher, even above storms. Submissive people can endure the storms when they understand the ways of God. This understanding gives them assurance about their immovable Rock.

Isaiah 40:31 says, "But they that wait upon the Lord shall renew their strength; they shall mount up with wings as eagles; they shall run, and not be weary; and they shall walk, and not faint." Submissive people must withdraw into Christ to be established on this immovable Rock. When they become established on and in Christ, He will become their strength. As these individuals are brought higher by Jesus' wisdom, they will also be enabled to reach deep into His immovable truths.

Finally, the eagle is fearless. Under the power of the Holy Spirit, submissive people can truly move in freedom. In fact, Jesus talked about how the wind cannot be controlled or understood. The wind is often symbolic of the Holy Ghost. Submissive people must step outside of their mind, and put their wings out in faith, and allow the wind of the Holy Ghost to lift them above the limited, earthly perspective to embrace God's perspective for the Body of Christ.

Are you submissive? Do you act like a turkey, or do you possess the intensity of an eagle who has an eternal perspective?

Are you living in your mind or are you soaring in the liberty of the Spirit?

The challenge for each Christian is to personally reflect Jesus to edify the Body and bring glory to God. In order to reach this potential, believers must come higher in their life in Christ.

12

EMITTING THE
FRAGRANCE OF CHRIST

2 Corinthians 2:14-16 says,

> Now thanks be unto God, which always causeth us to triumph in Christ, and maketh manifest the savour of his knowledge by us in every place. For we are unto God a sweet savour of Christ, in them that are saved, and in them that perish: To the one we are the savour of death unto death; and to the other the savour of life unto life. And who is sufficient for these things?

Obviously, the Church has what it takes to make a difference and conquer that which opposes it. Yet, many Christians appear to live in defeat. Is God's Word incorrect or are some of His people clearly missing it?

Any triumph a Christian might experience can only be found in Christ. This means that it is no longer the person who lives, but Christ lives in and through the believer.[1] It is Jesus' life that is powerful and attractive. It is His life that serves as a fragrance to God, the Church, and the world.

Therefore, Christ must be lifted up in each life in order to serve as an acceptable fragrance to God. This points to the voluntary sacrifices found in Leviticus 1-3. These sacrifices were not required like the sin and trespass offerings.[2] These sacrifices were freely given. They had to be anointed. As the fire consumed

---

[1] Romans 8:37; Galatians 2:20
[2] Leviticus 4 & 5

the sacrifice, the smoke and fragrance would ascend towards heaven. This smoke and fragrance brought pleasure to God.

Jesus served as a mandatory sin offering on the altar of the cross, but a voluntary sacrifice in His service before the Father, and toward others. As the Lamb of God His sacrifice was required by God to deal with our sin. Since Jesus became the mandatory offering, Christians, as part of His Body, are to serve as living sacrifices, constantly emitting a perpetual fragrance of His life to God. The living sacrifice points to a sacrifice that is being consumed by self-denial, the application of the cross, obedience to the Word, and the reality of Jesus. As the life of Jesus comes forth, it emits a fragrance that brings pleasure to God.

This fragrance also brings life to the Church. The life of Christ is the living bread that can be imparted to others for edification. His life is the light of man that can expose all sin, hindrances, and enemies. The life of Christ also points to resurrection life and power that enables one to be established in a relationship with the Living God. His life is the means to bring forth reconciliation between God and man.[3]

Finally, the fragrance of Christ's life signifies death to those who are unsaved. The unsaved are those who remain on the outskirts of God's salvation and reign. This fragrance becomes a harsh reality of judgment and wrath. Although the unsaved would like to brush the reality of Christ aside, this fragrance signifies His eternal life and becomes a haunting challenge.

Each Christian is called to express Jesus. Their lives must become the expression of His disposition. Their hearts must serve as an altar that constantly emits His fragrance, while their faith must become refined in their lives to bring them forth as priceless heirlooms that will crown Jesus' glorious head. Their dispositions must mirror or reflect His majesty. This is what it means for Christ

---

[3] John 1:3-11; 3:19-21; 6:35; Romans 6:1-9; 2 Corinthians 5:18-19

to be in all and to become all in all to those who name His Name as Lord and Savior.[4]

Scripture reveals what needs to happen for Christ to be unveiled in our lives before we begin to emit the fragrance of Christ for God's pleasure, the Church's edification, and a reality check to the unsaved. The greatest hindrance in emitting the fragrance of Jesus is self. Self wants to be honored and exalted as God. It wants to be served. It resents challenges, cries over adversity, and feels picked on when paying consequences. It wants the world to revolve around it, and failure to do so results in anger towards God and self-pity.

Self is forever avoiding personal accountability. In other words, self refuses to grow up and become responsible for personal attitudes and actions. Irresponsibility is an expression of what ails self—the desire to do nothing but what is convenient, comfortable, and feels good. It does not want to face the darkness, wickedness, and vanity of its ways. This is why it pursues fantasies that keep it from taking personal accountability. After all, if it has to face itself, it will have to be responsible to deny self, pick up the cross, and follow Jesus. Self expresses itself differently in each nature.

Submissive Nature

Submissive people can bring much needed heavenly perspective to the Church. The problem with these people is that until they become an eagle who soars on the wind of the Holy Spirit, they display an *unmanageable spirit*. When this natural spirit is in operation, these people become *self-absorbed*. Underneath self-absorption is complacency. This complacency wants nothing more than to be constantly satisfied so that it never has to stir itself up to do that which is uncomfortable. In other words, everything must be absorbed and made to submit or fit into mental

---

[4] Romans 8:29; 2 Corinthians 3:15-18; Galatians 2:20; Philippians 2:5

compartments to comply with their small worlds. When challenged to step into uncharted territories to properly confront reality, complacency responds in fake nobility. If the fake nobility fails to get the desired recognition, self-pity follows.

These people operate so much in their minds and self-absorbed worlds, that they begin to act more like turkeys who never get off the ground because they are stuck in their mental ruts. They are unable to get beyond their own conclusions, reality, and worldly wisdom to realize that they are not soaring above the situation; rather, they are buried by it.

Without a heavenly perspective, the Church will not have the wisdom of Christ. This means the pillars will be shaky rather than grounded on and in the Rock of Ages. Therefore, submissive people must get beyond their intellectual comfort zones and stir themselves up to explore the depths and heights of God. After all, they are meant to express the wisdom of Christ in confidence. This means they are reaching high to gain God's perspective, as they reach deep into His truths and ways. Such a pursuit will allow God to surround them with His perspective. Each time a submissive person is surrounded by His presence and glory, they begin to reflect God.

Sadly, the cords of fear and personal concepts bind many submissive people to their mental ruts. They do not know how to move beyond either to gain God's perspective. This keeps them from reaching their potential in Christ and emitting His fragrance to others. As a result, they fail to become the eagle. This condition simply means the submissive person will fail to reach great heights in God.

The heights of God allow submissive people to guard the ways of God with heavenly wisdom. This will edify the Church as these heights represent the victory of the cross, which comes by way of liberty in the Spirit.[5] As they are established in the ways of God, they become pillars that will uphold the ways and character of God. As pillars, submissive people will help others to discover the enduring, everlasting foundation of the Christian life: Jesus Christ.

This is why God cannot afford to let submissive people off the hook. He is calling them higher, but they must forget self by denying the credibility of their intellectual conceit and subduing their fear of facing and confronting life. They must exchange their natural, earthly wisdom for the heavenly wisdom from above.

The way that submissive people deny self is by choosing to love God with their entire *mind*.[6] This love will penetrate every compartment and override every concept. Once this occurs, the intense fleshly or worldly focus of these people will change from the earthly to the heavenly. The change will redefine their desire to understand the world around them with the need to know Jesus. As submissive people pursue the knowledge of Jesus, they will begin to soar in greater revelations of Him. Greater revelations of Jesus will give submissive people the authority to stand sure in the Body of Christ, as others seek wisdom and truth from their example.

When it comes to fear, submissive people must realize that it serves as an immovable wall. To overcome this fear, they must step back from the wall and look up towards the One who is able to draw near to them. Once these people stand back, look upward, and cry out for help, God can lift them out of their mental pit.

Revelation 1:9 says four things about the Apostle John. He was a brother, committed to the well-being of others in God's kingdom. He was a companion in tribulation, identified with others and capable of bringing consolation to those in despair. He was in the kingdom and patience of Christ, which meant he was an heir

---

[5] 2 Corinthians 3:17
[6] Mark 12:30

of salvation and identified with Christ in suffering and fruits. He was being <u>persecuted</u> for the Word of God and for the testimony of Jesus Christ.

As a pillar, John would not waver from the Word, and as an eagle, he had victory because of his testimony of Christ.[7] What a beautiful picture of the submissive person who is soaring in the heights of God, while firmly planted on the Rock. Such a person is trustworthy and reliable. These people can be immovable due to their foundation. Yet, they are unstoppable in regards to the heights they can reach in Christ because of the Holy Spirit.

Sometimes the Church tries to control or dictate the heights a submissive person is to reach in God. This is a grave error because it will close down or hinder the heavenly perspective. Perspective has to do with vision. This vision is in relationship to perspective outside of self and the Church. Keep in mind people without such vision will perish.[8]

If you are submissive, are you bound by fear or are you creating a mental rut? Are you a turkey, flopping around in the wind, or are you soaring with it like an eagle? Are you striving to reach the heights that God has prepared for you, so that you can bring a heavenly perspective to the Church regardless of what is going on in this world? Or, are you living in your own personal world? The answers to these questions will determine if you are reaching your potential in Christ, thereby, emitting His fragrance.

Stubborn Nature

The stubborn person has an *undisciplined spirit* until they become yoked with Jesus. It is very *selfish*; therefore, it insists that everything that enters its environment be designed for its personal use, needs, and desires. Selfishness often hides laziness. This

---

[7] Revelation 12:11
[8] Proverbs 29:18

laziness is indolent in attitude; therefore, it avoids anything that might result in pain or uneasiness. As a result, these people end up running in circles to avoid the reality that challenges their fantasies. If these people fail to properly face reality or allow their reality to be challenged, they become lazy and unreasonable. They will only act according to their emotions, and not according to reality and responsibility.

Stubborn people often refuse to grow up. They want their fantasy world. Their attitude is that they will either slide by or con their way around anything that does not serve their emotional purpose or come into compliance with the world they so desire. This is nothing more than laziness. Laziness reveals itself in rebellious attitudes and moodiness that leads to depression.

These people's unwillingness to face reality can be hidden behind their many excuses. They want everything to adjust to them, so they can feel good about themselves and their life. When they do not get their way, they become angry and rebellious. All too often, these people remain immature and foolish because they refuse to take responsibility for their emotions.

Stubborn people's undisciplined spirit can drive them mad with activities and endless commitments and pursuits. They naturally take on causes, but many of these causes have to do with making them feel better about self or creating the right environment. Once again, we see the need for these people to be yoked with Jesus, so that they can become like a tamed ox, a beast that will only shoulder the burdens put on by their Master. As the tamed ox, they will properly shoulder God's work, as well as always be ready to be offered up as an acceptable sacrifice for God's glory.

For most people, this type of disciplined life would not hold much significance. However, for the stubborn, it holds the key to liberty, purpose, and satisfaction. Although stubborn people fight to be free to do as they will, their need is to have their emotional momentum, aggression, and strength properly disciplined or channeled. They know if this strength is not properly channeled, it will prove to be chaotic and destructive for them. This is why they develop high *standards*.

These standards serve as their personal yoke that will bring what they consider to be the needed discipline to their environment. Rather than bringing discipline, these standards eventually cause overwhelming burdens that create a frustrating, condemning cycle.

The real conflict for stubborn people comes down to maintaining their freedom, while ensuring that their emotional strength is under proper control. Again, it comes down to the yoke they bear. If it is Christ's yoke, it will bring freedom through proper discipline.

This disciplined, sacrificial life does not point to fairness, but it does develop righteousness. It may not represent the free spirit that many stubborn people desire, but it does constitute the security that they so often seek and desire in their life. Like most people, what stubborn people often pursue is contrary to what they need to live a meaningful life.

It is hard for stubborn people to come to terms with godly discipline because they feel so deeply about their perception of their needs, as well as what is right and wrong and what would constitute real life to them. Yet, these deep feelings are what bring the greatest instability into their lives. This instability not only creates havoc for them, but also prevents them from serving as a fragrance to God, the Church, and the unsaved.

Stubborn people who are disciplined by the yoke of Jesus bring stability to the kingdom of God through bold leadership. They are meant to plow the way for the seeds of the Gospel to be planted in people's hearts. They prepare the way to the cross by example of an acceptable sacrifice. They establish other Christians in their faith as they serve as a plumb line to the righteous Cornerstone, Jesus Christ.

Therefore, God will not let stubborn people off the hook. They must become yoked with the One who became a sacrifice. This identification will give them the liberty to follow Jesus up the paths of righteousness. But, how do stubborn people submit to such rigid discipline? First, they must realize that Jesus' yoke is the only way that the Holy Ghost is able to produce in them a specific character or pattern of behavior. Until this character or pattern is established in stubborn people, they will always figure a way around paying the necessary price to become identified with Christ in every way. To avoid the price means they are avoiding the cross and identification.

Identification brings us to sacrifice. Stubborn people must sacrifice their need to be loved by choosing to love God with all of their *hearts*.[9] This sacrifice will align their affections towards heaven, thereby, changing their pursuits. As their affections become established in Christ, their life will become yoked with Him.

The yoke of Christ will channel stubborn people's emotional momentum in the right direction. They will plow up the hard turf of hearts, challenge conventional ways of man's religion, and display righteous indignation as they hold the line of righteousness against the works of wickedness.

Sadly, the Church fears stubborn people who display this momentum and righteousness. This fear causes those in position to try to control stubborn people's momentum. Ultimately, they muzzle the ox, preventing these people from being the prophetic voice in the Church. Silencing this voice could mean destruction for the Body, for this voice brings vital warnings and instructions.

People who encounter the bold leadership of a stubborn person must not try to muzzle them; rather, they must discern whether they are truly yoked with Christ and serving as His voice.

---

[9] Mark 12:29-31

If the stubborn person is yoked with Christ, stand back and let Jesus lead that individual where He desires. The results will not only prove to be interesting, but beneficial and necessary.

Are you stubborn? Are you yoked with Christ, bearing the burden of His kingdom, while always ready to be offered up as a sacrifice for His glory? If not, you will fail to reach your potential and serve as that incredible fragrance of Jesus. Remember the fragrance that is emitted comes out of sacrifice that is being burned by the purging fires on the altar.

Self-Assured Nature

Self-assured people have the highest potential in the kingdom of God. The reason is that they have the capability of reflecting the very image of Jesus. This means they have the ability to take on His disposition of a servant. Taking on a servant's disposition can only occur when self-assured people exchange their pursuit for perfection with the Lord's will. When this happens, these people can become an avenue by which Jesus' compassion is expressed, His fiercest leadership displayed, and His righteousness and purpose manifested to others.

The problem with self-assured people is that the ability to reflect Jesus is often enslaved by images, fear, and rebellion. These people have an *unyielding spirit* towards authority. Their unyielding spirit covers apathy that allows them to remain uncaring towards reality. This lack of concern enables them to maintain their pride or appearance of perfection no matter what it may cost them or others around them. Their unyielding spirit makes them *self-centered* and cruel. Self-centeredness demands that everything must be about them, and when it is exposed, it manifests itself in anger and vindictiveness.

These people, therefore, must totally yield everything to the Holy Ghost, but they often refuse to do so. Self-assured people will play the game in order to maintain their image and means of control. They will devise clever ways to avoid yielding their will or ways in order to hold on to their rights. They will substitute outward conformity for inward commitment. They will do anything except completely surrender.

Self-assured people's unwillingness to surrender prevents the Holy Ghost from completely sanctifying their body, soul, and spirit.[10] Without the work of sanctification, Jesus Christ will not be erected as the pillar or source in their life and reality. As a result, they will fail to reflect the image of Christ, do the will of the Father, and bring a consistent leadership to the Church. If Jesus is not erected, self-assured people will never become the anointed servant in God's kingdom. Without the anointing, they will never bring trustworthy or strong leadership to the Body. Ultimately, this will mar the part of the Body that serves as the crowning glory of God in a dark world.

The struggle for the self-assured person comes down to yielding or surrendering images, standards, rights, and life as they perceive each one. The aspect of surrendering is a terrifying prospect for these people. If yielding is a terrifying prospect or the last resort, how do self-assured people become a fragrance? The answer is obedience.

Godly obedience requires self-denial and submission. As self-assured people choose to obey, because it is the logical and righteous response, they will give way to the work of the Spirit. The Holy Ghost will begin to change their desires and pursuits as He sanctifies the different aspects of their character.

This brings us to the acceptable motivation. Godly obedience is a response of love.[11] Self-assured people must choose to love God with all of their *souls*. This means to obediently love Him at

---

[10] 1 Thessalonians 5:23
[11] John 14:15

the point of their wills, minds, and emotions. They must determine to do His will, to allow the Holy Ghost to develop Jesus' mind in them, and to permit the Spirit to channel their fierceness and authority as a means to produce compassion and consistency in their lives and leadership.

God will not let self-assured people off the hook. They must take on the full character of Christ. This means pride must give way to humility. Their independence must be replaced with meekness. They must submit their unyielding disposition to the Holy Ghost. They must exchange their images for God's will, and their defiance with the mind of Christ.

If self-assured people give way to the leadership of Jesus Christ, they will bring strong leadership to the kingdom of God. Sadly, many Christian practices encourage self-assured people to become enslaved to religious masks, façades, and games. Such slavery has marred the powerful reflection of Christ. As a result, self-assured people fail to sow the Gospel seed into hearts. They fall short of reflecting the product of the cross: the image of Christ in His unwavering love, commitment, and obedience. Without the ongoing reality of Christ, His life is never established inwardly. Without His reflection, His life will never be manifested outwardly in the Church or to the world.

If you are self-assured, make sure you yield or give way to the reality of God. This will ensure that you will reach your potential. Your life will serve as a fragrance that will please God, challenge the Church, and shake the foundation of the unsaved.

Strong-Willed Nature

Strong-willed people may be a lion in attributes, but they must become a lamb in disposition if they are going to become part of the fragrance of Christ to the Church and in this world. The biggest obstacle for strong-willed people is their *unruly spirit.*

The unruly spirit is very *self-serving*. It makes them obtuse or insensitive towards any reality that might challenge their sense of infallibility. Everything must adjust and line up to the strong-willed person's world. This need to rule causes strong-willed people to strive for control, so that they can rule their world in accordance to their reality. This is to ensure that everyone lines up to their reality in order to serve their purpose and reach their goals. They want people to automatically recognize their abilities, power, and authority, and submit. But, if people fail to do so, they will try to cage them into their world by playing games or bluffing their way to subdue and overwhelm. If their reality is consistently challenged, these people can become bullies who will make the person pay who refuses to line up to their way of thinking.

Their goals, power, and authority represent lines that bring them into competition with God, and serve as the means that will ultimately *cage* them into a rigid, unforgiving world that renders them useless to God. This closes down, perverts, or limits decisive leadership in His Body.

It prevents strong-willed people from preparing the way for the Gospel by bringing clarity and distinction to God's work and man's spiritual condition. These peoples' unruliness can keep them from showing the way and the work of the cross through example. Ultimately, they will fail to lead others to Christ to establish them on the right foundation and line them up to the Cornerstone.

For this reason, God will not let strong-willed people off the hook. They are a vital part of the Body and revelation of Jesus. To overcome their dominating nature, strong-willed people must become lambs in disposition. This disposition will bring godly leadership, discipline, and authority. Proper discipline will keep their sense of infallibility in the right perspective. It is this controlled disposition that will ultimately emit the fragrance of Christ.

To develop this disposition, strong-willed people must give way to the authority of God, and choose to love Him with all their *strength*.[12] They must allow the Rock of judgment to destroy their natural strength in order to embrace the reality of the complete work of Christ's redemption.

It is only as strong-willed people's strength is properly channeled that they become the strength and authority in the Church. Their strong, decisive leadership will bring confidence and direction to God's sheep. This clarity of leadership will prove that they have exchanged their personal crown of strength and authority with their personal cross. Such a cross points to regression. Regression in personal strength and confidence will develop the disposition of meekness and servitude. Application of their personal cross will mark their walk with straight, parallel lines, as they follow the King of kings.

Strong-willed people must, out of recognition of who God is, become lambs that follow the Lion of Judah. The meekness of a lamb will allow them to see their inability to do what is wise, righteous, and acceptable to God in the power of His Spirit. It will make them realize that all lasting accomplishments are a manifestation of His work and power.

Are you strong-willed? If so, are you a caged lion due to your cement lines or are you a lamb following the Shepherd? Are you striving for personal control and recognition, or have you given up your identity to press forward to the high calling in Christ Jesus? If you are failing to press forward, you will never become a fragrance acceptable to God, beneficial to the Church, or serve as an effective reality check to the doomed world.

---

[12] Mark 12:29-31

13

THE OVERCOMING CHURCH

Overcoming is not an option, but a visible expression of salvation. 1 John 5:4-5 confirms this, "For whatsoever is born of God overcometh the world: and this is the victory that overcometh the world, even our faith. Who is he that overcometh the world, but he that believeth that Jesus is the Son of God?"

In *Hidden Manna*, I have been revealing why Christians fail to overcome. They simply give into their fallen condition. In other words, they do that which is natural. For example, it is natural in our fallen condition to rebel against the authority of God. It is natural to resist, avoid, and ignore what is righteous when it does not properly fit into our comfort zones. It is natural to bow down to personal pride, justify the flesh, and compromise with the world. Since it is natural for carnal Christians to give way to their selfish disposition, they have a hard time perceiving why God would not see it their way and bless them in all of their religious attempts.

God's evaluation about the fallen condition of man is clearly recorded in the Scriptures. Sadly, our fallen condition blinds us to the fruits of our personal spiritual condition. We clearly see the ways of the flesh and the arrogance of pride in others, but we cannot see these active influences in ourselves. We actually remain indifferent to the personal devastation plaguing us from within.

Sadly, we cannot overcome until we come into line with God's evaluation of our fallen condition. We must recognize how our rebellion manifests itself, and our pride disguises itself. We must acknowledge how our flesh operates and the world affects us. Such enlightenment will mean the veil will fall off of our minds, so we can see the true face of our spiritual condition and properly respond to God.

One might wonder why people fail to see God's evaluation since it is clearly presented in Scripture. There are five reasons for this failure:

1) Due to pride, people must come out either as the savior or the victim in their world. In the kingdom of God, there is only one Savior, Jesus Christ, and there are no victims, just losers who refuse to pay the price of submission to know God. Pride refuses to acknowledge Jesus as Lord, and hides behind self-righteousness as it views the fleshly ways of others as ridiculous and foolish.

2) A person must have an open heart before God can reveal such matters to them. Hearts that are closed to God become hard towards those things that do not fit into their personal understanding.

3) Some people want to believe that there is still some good in them; therefore, they are deserving of blessings and happiness. But, if this were so, Jesus would not have had to die on the cross.

4) People want to believe that they are an exception to the Word rather than responsible to it. Subsequently, they are justified in ignoring it, claiming ignorance towards it, or disobeying it.

5) People do not want to take personal responsibility for their life, attitude, and practices; therefore, they operate in self-delusion and self-justification.

God must reveal the depth of our depravity, but we must be willing to look at it and agree with His evaluation. Such agreement lines us up to God's ways and thoughts. Once we come into a mental agreement with God's evaluation of our condition, we will begin to see the destructive path we are on, and turn from our way of doing and being to walk towards God. This is repentance.

Repentance is turning from our old way of living, and beginning to walk in the ways of obedience and righteousness before God. Obviously, without changing the direction of our walk to be converted to the ways of righteousness, we will never overcome.

Once the face of our fallen condition is revealed, we can give way to the work of the Spirit, resulting in regeneration and sanctification. God is able to begin the work of changing or regenerating us from within. This regeneration does not mean our nature is changed. Rather, it points to our traits being properly realigned as certain characteristics are mortified, and others are disciplined and channeled or sanctified by the Holy Ghost.

Obviously, to overcome, we must develop a relationship with God, rather than practice a religion. Each nature has a different way of expressing religion, while Jesus is clearly missing in their lives.

Submissive people major in knowledge about the Word, rather than coming to the knowledge of the Living Word, Jesus. This makes Christianity a religion of controllable facts and formulas, rather than a relationship. Jesus becomes a *concept* that is complimented by the uniqueness of the Word of God with all of its facts, history, and spiritual insights. However, this knowledge never gets past the mind. Since it stops at the mind, submissive people can remain indifferent about the reality around them, including their own spiritual condition.

To ensure that Jesus becomes real, submissive people must recognize that their conclusions do not represent the wisdom or truth from heaven. They must bring all thoughts into captivity and into obedience to Jesus, and begin to seek Him out as the Living Word in order to possess Him as a *living* and *personal Savior.*[1]

Since minds serve as their personal lord over submissive people's reality, they must step past their minds and make the Person of Jesus, Lord. This is a hard battle for them because while they are struggling in their minds to not go into their minds, they become weary and overwhelmed. They cannot imagine themselves functioning outside of their minds. It is as though they first must run out of compartments and options before Jesus can step on the scene and lift them out of their endless mental pit.

Stubborn people often create a Jesus according to their emotional feelings. This Jesus becomes a contradiction of religious notions as He is constantly being adjusted to present emotions or environments. For example, they perceive Him as loving, but if He fails to perform according to their feelings, they conclude He does not love them. Sadly, the Jesus these people create is nothing more than an unrealistic fantasy or a harsh, unloving Savior that is unfair, prejudicial, and who appears to constantly toy with people's emotions.

When Jesus fails to prove His undying love for them according to their standards, they put up a wall of skepticism against Him. Skepticism causes them to play the religious game by becoming religious, dogmatic, and legalistic in their beliefs. They become plagued with doubts and pushed by self-righteousness, causing them to become judgmental towards others. Ultimately, they will perceive themselves to be suffering martyrs.

The Jesus whom stubborn people often erect is fickle and weak in crisis, uncertainties, and changes. This is why they must know Jesus as a *Powerful Savior* who cannot be controlled by emotional whims or changes according to environments. His life and ways prove that He remains the same, and that nothing can

---

[1] John 1:1; 2 Corinthians 10:5

sway Him from Who He is and His commitment to His followers.[2] Since emotions serve as the master of stubborn people, they must allow God's Word to master or discipline their emotions, as they choose to allow it to serve as their final authority.

Stubborn people must also avoid taking Jesus' "so-called" failure to comply with their standards and whims as personal rejection. Jesus' proof of His love for each of us can be seen by His own sacrifice on the cross. Therefore, it is not up to Him to wade through the endless parade of a person's emotions to prove His commitment when He has already done so on the cross.

Self-assured people erect an image of Jesus that serves as their personal religious image. This image of Jesus is not realistic because it lacks His disposition. For example, self-assured people see Jesus as a perfect image, but not as a perfect Man who truly lived and breathed. The key to Jesus' perfection as man was His disposition as a servant. He was totally yielded to the will of the Father. Without the reality of this disposition, both the face and spirit behind Jesus would be changed as He is robbed of His humanity and made unobtainable or untouchable by mere man.

Once self-assured people bring down the religious image, they can accept Jesus' work of grace as the *Perfect Savior* on the cross in order to make Him Lord of their life. They will see that all He does in His followers' lives is a matter of grace and not a situation where they obtain some personal level of perfection.

Strong-willed people make Christianity a matter of facts that are shaped according to their personal understanding. They see Christ as black and white, but there is no dimension or personality to Him. A person's disposition serves as the reflection of someone's character, but personality is how a person will manifest their disposition. Therefore, without this dimension or personality,

---

[2] Hebrews 13:8

Jesus remains an idea to strong-willed people, rather than a living reality.

This allows strong-willed people to be indifferent to spiritual matters or concepts. They often act outside of religious matters or beliefs in order to reshape them according to their perceptions. Their lifeless perceptions of Jesus make their life before God not only religious, but also controllable. Jesus inevitably becomes someone who can be understood and reshaped to fit the situation. In other words, they are always trying to fit God and His activities into their world.

It is vital that strong-willed people come to terms with Jesus as their *Promised Savior*. Promise points to something that will be accomplished. This not only implies action, but a certainty or reality. Jesus not only came as the Promised Messiah and suffering Savior the first time, but He is coming back as the victorious King and Lord. These people need to realize that everything about their life in Christ must line up between these two decisive realities about Jesus.

For example, strong-willed people must line up their ideas to who Jesus is. They must allow Him to become Lord in their activities, the Anointed One in ministering to others, and the only Savior in light of redemption. After all, strong-willed people always try to figure out how to save the day to bring their world into order and under control. Such a pursuit is often driven by their need to receive recognition and honor from those around them. They need to give this need for recognition to God in worship and to others in ministry.

Once the relationship with God is on track, each person must come to terms with how their flesh operates.

The Flesh

The flesh represents the natural tendencies or inclinations of the fallen condition. When a person understands how the flesh operates, they can get a small glimpse of how far the unregenerate disposition is from the glory of God. It is overwhelming, sobering, and frightening. In fact, the reality of this could drive people mad if they fail to understand it in light of God's forgiveness. God's forgiveness does not take away the sorrow or despair that such a personal revelation can bring, but it does offer hope in spite of it. This hope leads to God's provision of salvation.

The first factor we must recognize about the flesh is that it refuses to submit to any authority. It will devise games to get around authority. These games give an impression of obedience and humility, while maintaining the rights of the flesh to call the shots, as well as determine the terms of what it will subject itself to.

These games are deceptive, but they serve as a point of control and manipulation. They feed pride in order to use people. They flatter in order to reign. These games toy with people's emotions in order to control. They lack integrity, but many play them in the name of harmony, family, personal agendas, and success.

These games toy with souls as they wrap up lives and the world in a perverted reality. In spite of how many Christians justify such games, they are fleshly and worldly. They avoid or oppose the work of the Spirit. This opposition puts them in the ways of separation from God and spiritual ruin. Therefore, how can a person know if they are operating in the flesh or walking by the Spirit?

Submissive people can automatically know they are operating in the flesh when they withdraw into their minds to seek wisdom, understanding, and direction. God does not speak to the mind, for it will pervert or limit the effects of His truth. Rather, He speaks to a person's spirit. Once a truth reaches into the spirit of a person, it will enlarge their mind to embrace the truth. This is why submissive people must know that their conclusions outside of God's perspective are fleshly and untrustworthy. They must avoid *complying,* not only to their mental ruts, but also with those in their world. These people must choose to hold all conclusions lightly and bring all of their thoughts into obedience to Jesus.[3]

Stubborn people can know that they are operating in the flesh when they give way to their emotions. These people are always trying to *reform* themselves and their environment to get their emotional needs met. Many stubborn people perceive that these emotions are from the heart. This is incorrect. These emotions are operating according to the appetites of the flesh and the vain imaginations of the mind. Stubborn people must remember how fickle and unrealistic the reality can prove to be that are created by their undisciplined emotions.

When stubborn people begin to recognize that their emotions are beginning to escalate, they must avoid going there. After all, it does not take much for these people to fall victim to the tidal waves of their emotions. All they have to do is take their emotional temperature. Since they feel deeply about a matter, they will feel justified going with the momentum and conclusions of their undisciplined emotions. The only source that can bring a proper reality to their undisciplined emotions is the Word and character of God. Therefore, stubborn people must make a heart determination to believe God, rather than allow their emotions to reign.

Self-assured people who walk according to the reality of their images are simply giving in to the flesh. These people will *perform* according to their images to get desired responses. However,

---

[3] 2 Corinthians 10:5

images are in competition with God and unrealistic. Those who walk according to their fragile reality or images are trying to reach maturity or perfection in their own strength.

These people will fail miserably in their attempt to be perfect, but sadly those around them pay for their inability to reach this perfect state. Frustration, anger, bitterness, and hatred often flow out from self-assured people towards others.

When *strong-willed* people rely upon their facts or ideas, they are operating in the flesh. The works of the flesh are expressed in their need to control their world. They resort to different methods to gain the desired control. They first try playing a game or adjusting to the situation. They do this by *conforming* to a situation. They may approach a situation from different angles, always adjusting their approach or maneuvers. But, the motivation behind all of these attempts is to win confidence so they can gain control. If this doesn't work, they can display self-pity or become aggressive and intimidating because of frustration and anger.

God will not bow down to the understanding of the submissive person, wade through the emotions of the stubborn, or compete with the images of the self-assured to try to bring a person to truth. He will never adjust so that He can fit into the world of strong-willed people, nor will He allow Himself to be defined and controlled by their facts or lines. It is up to each individual to recognize the operation of the flesh in their life, and to step outside of the destructive cycle.

This brings us to the next area that must be properly examined: that of the spirit.

The Motivation

People are always judging others by their outward conformity, rather than discerning their spirit. We are told that we can only interact with God from the premise, influence, and leading of the

Holy Spirit. However, there are three main spirits in operation in the world. There is the Spirit of God, but each person also has a natural spirit that operates in them. If the individual does not discipline or rule their spirit, they will become like an unwalled city that is broken down and will not have the walls of safety to properly protect them. This brings us to the third spirit, which is of this present world. We know the god of this world is Satan. He is the prince that rules the unseen kingdom that opposes God and works within those who are disobedient.[4]

It is vital to understand how spirit works. It motivates the different attitudes and approaches of a person. It determines the intent or purpose behind an individual's activities. It will determine what each of us comes into agreement with, as well as personal preferences and attractions. It actually sets up the inner and outer environments in which people operate. The spirit behind people's motivation and intent will manifest itself in the fruits that will be produced in their lives.

Needless to say, the unchecked natural spirit of man and the spirit of the world represent the wrong spirits. They are motivated by the same source, as well as possess the same intent, goals, and fruits. If man's spirit is not properly ruled, Satan will find the necessary inroads to oppress the soul of man or possess his spirit, soul, and body.

These wrong spirits must be properly confronted in order to overcome the flesh and Satan. For example, the natural spirit will toy with sin, justify it, and give way to its temptation. As a result, a person must repent to bring the natural spirit into subjection to the Holy Spirit. Satan throws well aimed darts at our minds, such as lies to confuse us. In such confusion he is able to seduce a person into another reality. James 4:1-10 tells us about the types of influence the flesh and the world has on each of us, and what it

---

[4] Proverbs 25:28; 2 Corinthians 4:3-4; Ephesians 2:2-3; 1 John 4:1

will take to overcome such influences. Repentance results in cleansing, while submitting ourselves unto God will cause Satan to flee. In other words, we take authority over him by coming under the authority of God. Sadly, people often repent of what Satan is behind, and try to take authority over their flesh. The wrong response simply keeps people in bondage. This is why we must discern the spirit that is in operation.

Consider the following table. Notice the fruits or end result that is produced by the different spirits in operation.

Spirit	Right Spirit	Wrong Spirit
Motivation	Love of God	Pride
Intention	Glorify God	Honor self
Goal/ Focus	Lift Jesus Up	Make self God
Results	Liberty in the Spirit/Fruit of the Spirit	Must control reality, ends in bondage

Clearly, we must learn how to not only discern the spirit behind others, but the spirit we are operating in. Sadly, most of us unfairly judge others, while justifying ourselves. There is a difference between judging and discerning. Judging is based on the flesh and is opinionated, bigoted, and dogmatic. Such judging will come down to how someone makes a person feel about their world. If a person rattles another person's world in any way, it will result in the one who has been offended judging the culprit.

Discerning is wading through the outward influences to determine the spirit or motivation of someone. The ability to discern depends on one's sensitivity to the Holy Ghost, and a balanced understanding of the intent or spirit behind the Word of God. The flesh will never discern, while discernment will not allow the things of the flesh to affect its ability to righteously evaluate the type of spirit behind something.[5]

The motivation of the selfish disposition is pride. This is the essence of self. When a person is not under the right spirit, they are operating according to personal concepts, standards, images, or ideas. These *rulers* make the individual the ultimate authority and judge concerning matters. These rulers also serve as a door through which the spirit of the world, Satan, can come in and reinforce lies, fears, and rebellion.

Submissive people who are operating under the wrong spirit become *unmanageable.* An unmanageable spirit can escalate into an impenetrable state where the person becomes *pigheaded.* Initially, this state expresses itself in attitudes. In other words, these people become obnoxious or closed down. Both scenarios prevent truth or reasoning from *penetrating* this person's reality. In fact, when a submissive person is closed, it is like hitting an immovable wall. The immovable wall of submissive people is fear. Fear allows this person to ignore or live in denial about what is

---

[5] 1 Corinthians 2:14

going on around them. Either way, people have a hard time penetrating through the obnoxious bristles or the immovable wall of a submissive person who is out of balance or control.

Stubborn people become totally *unreasonable* when they are operating under a wrong spirit. Their unreasonableness makes them *bullheaded.* They will run over you verbally, or take you around the mountain over and over with their endless excuses. In extreme cases, you will hit an immovable wall of skepticism that often hides fear, rejection, betrayal, and anger.

Self-assured people become *cruel* and *mule-headed* when they are operating under a wrong spirit. This cruelty comes out of their pride or the need to be right. It serves as a wall that will prevent anything from challenging their reality. They can be verbally or physically abusive during this time, while justifying any action taken in order to survive and come out on top.

Strong-willed people become *formidable* when they are operating in a wrong spirit. They become *hard-headed* about what they perceive as being right. In a way, they become unstoppable, regardless of the destruction that may follow them. At this point, these people are often being driven by fear. Their life is totally out of control, and all of their attempts to gain control have fallen to the wayside. Now, fear is about to consume them and they will run, especially in their minds, to figure out how to silence this taunting fear. In fact, these people become their own worst enemy as they teeter on the edge of insanity.

It is noteworthy to understand what opens people up to the wrong spirit. There are three elements that serve as open doors to a wrong spirit. They are:

Rebellion
Control
Reality

Rebellion is a product of pride. Pride will always open people up to a wrong spirit. This is why James 4:7 tells us to, "Submit yourselves therefore to God. Resist the devil, and he will flee from you."

Control can become a form of witchcraft. An example of witchcraft is when someone tries to exert their will over another person's will. This is where games come into the picture. People often play games to get their way through a type of seduction. Some people are professional about it, but the resentment, treachery, anger, and breakdown of trust and relationships that follow are the byproducts of such control.

Reality is a big issue with most people. God cannot bring truth into a situation that is devoid of reality. He cannot bring instruction when one is in denial of their personal reality. He cannot bring liberty as long as one is trying to adjust personal reality to fantasy. The truth is most people cannot stand their present reality; therefore, they do everything within their means to change it. When reality actually challenges a person's desired reality, fear and anger follow. This state will eventually produce depression.

The final area that must be considered is the heart condition. After all, the issues of life originate in the heart.[6]

The Heart Condition

People have a hard time coming to terms with their heart. First of all, it is deceitful.[7] This means people cannot trust the intent of the heart because self often sits on the throne of the heart and reigns in utter delusion.

Jesus said of the heart that all sin originates with it. Once again, at the core of sin is self. When self reigns, the flesh is in operation. When the flesh is in operation, it serves as a covering

---

[6] Proverbs 4:23
[7] Jeremiah 17:9-10

that blinds and perverts a person to the things of God, making it impossible to discern spiritual matters.[8]

The fleshly covering is a veil of unbelief. It actually prevents the things of God from penetrating a person's spirit.[9] In other words, the flesh circumvents the heart. When spiritual matters or truths are perverted and kept from penetrating a person's heart, these individuals will remain unchanged in the inner man.

When the right spirit is missing, people will make their Christian life into a religion. They will dress up the works of the flesh in religious garb. They will outwardly try to rehabilitate the old man, as self piously reigns unhindered and unchallenged from the heart. And, as long as self reigns, the heart will remain untouched by the Spirit. It will remain uncircumcised and far away from God.[10] The main fruit of such a heart will be disobedience.

There is only one reason God's people obey Him in spirit and truth: Because they love Him. Jesus made this clear in John 14:15, "If ye love me, keep my commandments."

The Apostle John reiterated this point in 2 John 6, "And this is love, that we walk after his commandments. This is the commandment, that, as ye have heard from the beginning, ye should walk in it."

Sadly, people trip over the first commandment because they do not choose to seek God with the commitment to love and serve Him with all of their heart.[11] They become religious or obsessed with the "supernatural," while God remains a controllable belief.

Godly love cannot remain indifferent. It must respond to the one who is loved. It cannot ignore cries, pleads, or needs. It cannot justify indifference, abuse, cruelty, or tyranny. It must respond in

---

[8] Matthew 15:16-20; 1 Corinthians 2:14
[9] 2 Corinthians 3:14-15; 4:3-6
[10] Matthew 15:3-9; Hebrews 4:12; 10:14-17
[11] Mark 12:19-31

commitment, uphold matters in righteousness, and obey that which is honorable in humility and submission.

Many Christians fail to fall in love with God. They may fall in love with their concepts about Him and get caught up with their emotions towards Him. They may become impressed with their images concerning Him, and become confident in their ideas about Him, but they fail to fall in love with the Person of God. And, when that love is missing, so is the reality or manifestation of Christ's attitude and life.

Christianity is a matter of the heart. Everything must be done from a heart that has sanctified or set God apart in devotion and service. This heart must be single in focus, consistent in desire, and unwavering in faith. It must be totally compelled and consumed by the love of God and a love for God.[12]

How do these four natures circumvent their hearts, so that they remain untouched and unchanged by God and His Word? *Submissive* people resort to their mind. This prevents the truth of God from penetrating their hearts as it is carefully processed. By operating in their minds, they can control reality. They comply outwardly to the things of God, while deeming their personal conclusions as being wise. Usually, they are very impressed with their conclusions or knowledge, and see their so-called wisdom as a way of bringing them *honor*. Meanwhile, they become *complacent* towards personal problems and issues around them.

This allows them to *ignore* reality as they conclude that everything will eventually turn out okay down the road. Such a conclusion allows them to become so *self-absorbed* that they end up being clueless to problems in their lives and families, allowing their conclusion to gain momentum. Since they ignore reality, very few issues are resolved. Unresolved issues create a tidal wave

---

[12] Romans 5:5; 2 Corinthians 5:14; Ephesians 6:5-6; 2 Timothy 2:19-22; 1 Peter 3:15

that will eventually wreak havoc in their lives. Needless to say, this indifference will cause delusion.

Submissive people need to give the *honor* they secretly desire to others. This will help them to come down from the intellectual pinnacles of their minds, and allow God's truths to penetrate their hearts. As His truth and love penetrate their hearts, they will begin to show proper consideration for others. They will become sensitive to others, allowing them to effectively minister to them.

Stubborn people circumvent their hearts by keeping reality on an emotional level. They often confuse their deep emotions with their heart; therefore, presuming that those things that are deeply affecting them are a matter of the heart. Therefore, they mistake their emotions as truth. As already stated, emotions are a matter of the flesh, and must come into subjection to the Word of God before they can be properly challenged.

By operating in their emotions, stubborn people create a fantasy that causes them to live in *denial* about their present reality. This fantasy keeps them from facing reality; therefore, truth is never allowed to penetrate their hearts. When reality does challenge them, unbalanced, stubborn people become angry because others have failed to bow down to their illusions to bring forth their desired reality.

This brings us to another important point about stubborn people. Because of their need and their emotional makeup, they desire to receive *adoration*. Therefore, when people fail to bow down to their illusions, they also fail to show the proper adoration towards them. As you can see, this emotional merry-go-round is not only confusing and unrealistic, but it can be insane.

Stubborn people must give up their need to be understood, and give that understanding to others. These people can be very compassionate and giving. However, when they are circumventing their hearts, they often distribute unfeeling criticism to those who fail to bow down to their standards or illusions.

Self-assured people circumvent their hearts by changing images. By changing images, reality can be adjusted. Therefore, they never have to deal with the reality of their actions and become accountable to those in their world. Since their images are devoid of emotions, they can be indifferent to others' feelings. They can ignore other people's struggles because perfection is a matter of changing an image and not a matter of a changed heart. Ultimately, these people can become a harsh *judge* of what constitutes reality as they seek *glorification* for their images.

Self-assured people need to get past their images and begin to recognize the humanity of others. Instead of being an ultimate judge of humanity, they need to become identified with it. Instead of trying to lord over others, they need to become a true servant to all. Instead of seeking glorification, they need to lift up Jesus in His glory so others can be drawn to Him.[13]

Strong-willed people circumvent their heart by keeping reality a matter of facts. These facts establish concrete ideas. These ideas are considered infallible. Therefore, these ideas make these people *insensitive or hard* to that which does not fit into their controlled worlds.

Since strong-willed people perceive their facts as being infallible, they expect others to pay *homage* to them. This homage is their idea of showing proper recognition for their intelligence, abilities, and actions.

These people need to take their need for recognition and start giving it to God in service and to others in ministry. They need to give God permission to shake their ideas in order to make them pliable in His hands.

As you can see, the heart is always circumvented at the point where self is preferred, exalted, and treated as God. This is the

---

[13] John 12:32

hidden agenda behind all unregenerate human nature. Only God deserves honor, adoration, glorification, and homage.

The problem with self being in the position of God is that it is not God. It is contrary to the very nature of God. Its so-called truth is nothing more than perverted reality. And, that which demands service is nothing more than idolatrous flesh. Its insatiable ego wants to be flattered or honored as it reserves the right to prostitute itself with the world without consequences or judgment.

Self strives to be God. And, when self reigns, God will be nothing more than a religious belief. When self reigns, there is no room to love God, because one is in love with self. When self reigns, it desires all worship and adoration. And, when self reigns, there is no room for others to be regarded, considered, or preferred.

What about you? Consider the following table on the next page and see if self is reigning in all of its vainglory, or if God is reigning in all of His majesty.

Types	Submissive	Stubborn	Self-Assured	Strong-Willed
Gospel	John	Mark	Luke	Matthew
Symbol	Eagle	Ox/Calf	Man	Lion
Point of Subjection	Mind	Heart	Soul	Strength
Type of Bondage	Bound	Muzzled	Enslaved	Caged
Natural Spirit	Unmanageable (Complacent)	Undisciplined (Lazy)	Unyielded (Apathetic)	Unruly (Obtuse)
Wrong Spirit	Impenetrable (Pigheaded)	Unreasonable (Bullheaded)	Cruel (Mule-headed)	Formidable (Hardheaded)
Type of Self-Exaltation	Self-absorbed	Selfish	Self-centered	Self-serving
Types of Games Played	Compliant to get way.	Reforming to get way.	Performing to get way.	Conforming to get way.
Agenda	To be honored	To be adored	To be glorified	To be paid homage
Substitution of Jesus	Religious Concept	Religious Notion	Religious Image	Controlled Fact
Jesus, the Rock	Foundation	Cornerstone	Erected, Anointed Pillar	Rock of Judgment
Jesus As Savior	Living, Personal Savior	Powerful Savior	Perfect Savior	Promised Savior
Responsibility In Church	Vision/ Perspective	Prophetic Voice	Image of Christ	Authority

14

A FINAL THOUGHT

My greatest challenge in writing a book is knowing how to start and finish it. This book is no exception. Since my books emphasize the reality of God, I realize there is no good beginning or ending when it comes to His infinite character and ways. He is so faithful to continue to unveil the depths of His character, and to reveal the incredible mercy, grace, and faithfulness He shows to those who desire to know, love, and serve Him.

This book is a revision because He has given me more insight into human nature. In doing so, He has also revealed His Son in greater measure. This is necessary, because without Jesus, there is no balance to man's world.

There is a well-known story about a man who cut up a picture of the world and gave it to his son to put it back together. Surprisingly, the boy accomplished the task quickly. When the father asked the boy how he managed this feat in such a short time, the little boy showed him that there was a picture of Jesus on the other side. He had simply put the world back together by putting together the picture of Jesus.

The *Hidden Manna* information has an incredible history. Back in 1977, the Lord impressed upon me as a new Christian that He had a book for me to write. At the time, I was attending college and felt a real leading to cease my college pursuits and go home. Many questioned my move, but I can see how God wanted to keep my slate clean from the influence of liberal secular education.

In the next seven years, I took many detours in my Christian life, only to end up broken at His feet. It was at that vulnerable time that He began an incredible process in me. This process meant breaking down my preconceived notions about Him and religion. Once my notions were brought down, He could begin to write on my slate the truth about His character, as well as reveal my spiritual state.

It was a bittersweet time for me. He stripped away layers to reveal certain aspects of my selfish disposition, while revealing His love, forgiveness, and commitment to my spiritual well-being. I did not understand the significance of that balance until later when I realized that my life could not be put back together until Jesus was clearly revealed in greater ways to my heart.

The truth is man has no identity outside of Christ. The Bible clearly states that our life is in Him and He is in us. Over the years, I have grown to appreciate that little word "in" as it continually stipulates in Scripture my relationship, position, and identity in Christ.

It was not until 1986 that God began to reveal the *Hidden Manna* information. I can see where He gave me a gift of faith to simply believe and pursue the information out of a child-like curiosity and trust. He then gave me a co-laborer in the Gospel, Jeannette, who would also share in testing out and discovering new insights into human nature. I had no idea where it was all leading me, but I sense that it was a valuable tool that could edify others.

In 1995, *Hidden Manna,* the book, finally was published and the first copy sold April 8th. The Lord had impressed upon me that this is the book He wanted me to write. I had my challenges in writing. My English was horrific and caused nightmares for those who tried to edit it. I was also struggling under a barrage of various obstacles that caused me to consider giving up the idea of a book altogether and simply use it as a personal tool in ministry.

As I held my first copy of *Hidden Manna*, it struck me that it represented an 18-year spiritual odyssey. The odyssey began with a zealous ignorance of God, but ended with an incredible revelation of Jesus.[1] Suddenly, it dawned on me how faithful God had been to bring me down a particular course. This whole journey was not about a book. Rather, it was about my own spiritual growth. Even though I had considered some of my experience as a total nightmare, I realized that I had discovered, and was beginning to possess the Great Prize of Jesus Christ.

When it began to dawn on Jeannette and me how powerful this information was, we wanted the whole world to know about it. Surprisingly, God kept it hidden. This puzzled me. I wrestled with this issue until He revealed to me how people take that which is precious and pure to Him and simply add it to the smorgasbord of information they already have in order to feed their already growing intellectual pride. Or, they would defile, abuse, and use it for their personal gain.

Sadly, I have witnessed people take this information and use it to control and manipulate others. In other cases, I have watched "wannabe" ministers see this information as a means to exalt themselves in His kingdom. Even though this information is simple, it is profound and only those with sincere hearts can properly grasp it. And, even those who have a balanced understanding of it admit they could never do it justice by teaching it.

The *Hidden Manna* information also proved to be controversial. It was often associated with self-help information, the four temperaments, or psychology. I never realized that so many Christians had lost their way and were now seeking means outside of Christ to find their way back to some purpose or meaning. Any time self is promoted, Christ will be missing.

---

[1] Romans 10:2-3

As far as the four temperaments information is concerned, I discovered it had ties with the New Age, while the roots of psychology can be traced back to the occult. It was not unusual to immediately encounter one of two attitudes: "I already know the information" or "you are in error!" At times I felt I was walking through a minefield. I never knew when I was going to meet with conceit or skepticism and criticism.

I began to wonder why God would even bother to reveal this information in the midst of these controversies, abuses, and misuses. I even wrestled with God about this predicament. Was I meant to keep it to myself and just use it in ministry? Was it really from God or some terrible joke from Satan who played on my innocence and sincerity?

The questions and examinations flooded my soul. Through it all, I was constantly reminded of how the information helped people and remained consistent under my constant examination, as well as the scrutiny of those who bothered to test it. Truth will not change no matter how it is tested. But, the question as to why God would even bother to unveil this information at this time in history when the world as we know it is winding down to a climactic end, continued to challenge the recesses of my mind.

Surprisingly, God seemed to reveal to me the answer to this question. As never before in history, man is searching for his identity and purpose. One wonders why man is so caught up with the concept of self. Is it because he has come to the end of his other pursuits and found them all to be vain? Is it because he has more time to focus on himself?

Whatever the reason, it seems that man is trying to discover the source of his plight by looking inward. He perceives that if he can understand himself, he will come to terms with his world. However, in his search, he avoids seeking out God, and turns to the world's philosophies and doctrines of demons.

Why would man avoid seeking for his Creator? As I studied different philosophies that people pursue, I noticed the absence of one main issue: **Sin**. For example, self-help programs give the impression that man can change his world by simply pulling up his bootstraps and applying certain formulas. The temperament information puts the pressure on people to recognize their temperament, thereby, changing their atmosphere. Psychology explains destructive behavioral patterns according to the past. It often puts the blame of people's destructive patterns and actions on others.

Needless to say, the problem to the plight of man has not changed since man's rebellion in the Garden of Eden. The problem remains the same. It comes down to sin. Sin can only be revealed in the light of a Holy God. Sin is not taken care of by hiding it behind a cloak, ignoring it, justifying it, or denying its very existence. It can only be dealt with in one way—at the foot of Jesus' cross.

The harsh reality is that man needs forgiveness for his sins, healing from its workings in his life, and restoration from its various activities in order to come to terms with the significance of his life and purpose. Man cannot find this forgiveness by shifting the blame, looking inward, or towards some type of relationship and philosophy. He can only find lasting resolutions for his life when he steps outside of self and beyond all relationships and philosophies of the world.

This brings us to *Hidden Manna*. Much of the popular information in regards to the plight of man offered to Christendom is weak, worldly, or heretical. It is meant to appeal to the ignorant, arrogant, and the superficial. It is designed to sell books rather than save souls. It is capable of whetting fleshly appetites, but incapable of satisfying the soul. It offers formulas, but not lasting eternal solutions. It gives the impression of doing spiritual surgery when all it does is put a Band-Aid on a bleeding artery. It uses

Christianity as a platform to present and sell ideas that lack both spirit and truth, often merchandising souls in the end.

In spite of this poor, weak, erroneous presentation, God is faithful. He always presents the truth in the midst of error to bring contrast and challenge. Because of people's search for self and the inundation of substandard and heretical information, He simply raised up a standard of righteousness by unveiling the true identity of man. Man's problem has not changed—it is called "sin". His solution remains the same—The Lord Jesus Christ.

Many people have become depressed by the *Hidden Manna* information because it takes the glamour out of human nature to reveal the harsh reality of man's fallen condition. People begin to see their rebellion, pride, and self-exaltation. They start to realize how they strive to become god in order to determine truth and maintain personal control and reality. Some have even whined and complained about how this information does not leave their particular nature in a good light. It cannot be denied. This information unveils the harsh reality of sin. However, this harsh reality was meant to bring people to one conclusion: They need to be delivered from themselves, and there is only One person who can accomplish such a feat. His name is the Lord Jesus Christ.

Man cannot understand or change his world by looking within. For his world to make sense and be put back together, Jesus Christ must become a living reality to him. For his life to take on meaning and purpose, Jesus must be lifted up in his life. For His life to make a difference, he must become an extension of Jesus Christ as he manifests His attitude, life, and examples to others.

Hidden Manna does nothing more than bring people back to basic scriptural truths. This information reveals sin, calls for repentance, and lifts up Jesus as the only solution. It calls for self-denial, application of the cross, and obedience to Jesus. It unveils Jesus in the midst of His creation. This is no different than what

God's Word has done. Therefore, why write a whole book to bring out these truths when they are clearly outlined in the Word of God?

Sadly, Christianity has been inundated with an endless stockpile of nonsense that has become a detour from these simple truths. This nonsense subtly puts the focus back on man, rather than on God. As long as man is the emphasis, God will never become the solution. The purpose of *Hidden Manna* is to reverse this emphasis by showing people that their endless search for self will bring them to a hopeless abyss. And, it's when man reaches this abyss of nothingness, that is when he will most likely look upward to the only One who can put his world back together. It is when man finds Christ and allows Him to take His rightful place as King and Lord in his life that he will discover his true identity and purpose.

Although *Hidden Manna* gives valuable insight into the four natures found within humanity, it brings people back to their need for God to find forgiveness, restoration, and to overcome, and to reach their potential in Christ. It unveils Jesus in the midst of humanity, thereby, giving people a vision beyond themselves to see a greater eternal significance for their existence.

I realized that *Hidden Manna* was God's way of making the truth available in the midst of the weak and heretical substitutes. Many people have been blessed and helped by this information. But, to me, the greatest asset is not the insight about human nature, but the revelation of Jesus Christ. He is the Manna hidden within veiled humanity, and He can only be perceived and embraced by those who have the spiritual eyes to see and the ears to hear.

As I come to the end of this book, I realize that it is not my responsibility to make sure God's people are exposed to this information. My job was to write a book in order for Him to make it available to those He chooses to reveal it to. After all, *Hidden*

Manna is His information and has been dedicated to Him for His use and glory.

I am both thankful and awed that He has revealed this information to me. It has allowed me to discover how wonderful He is. It has given me a vision beyond self, and set me free to soar in the wonderment and beauty of His love, grace, power, and majesty.

My prayer is that each reader will have the eyes and ears to truly see Jesus in this book. After all is said and done, at the end of every great spiritual odyssey is the glorious reality of the King of kings and the Lord of lords. It is only as Jesus arises as the bright and morning star within man's soul that it becomes obvious that He is man's only great hope in which to discover the promised life and his ordained potential and purpose in light of heaven's eternal purpose and glory.

Bibliography

Strong's Exhaustive Concordance of the Bible; World Bible Publishers.

Vine's Expository Dictionary of Biblical Words; © 1985 by
    Thomas Nelson, Inc., Publishers

Webster's New Collegiate Dictionary; © 1976, G. & C. Merriam Co.

The 1st Church of the Program by Robert L. Rees, article

Jewish Faith and the New Covenant; Ruth Specter Lascelle; © 1980

The Power of the Spirit; William Law; © 1971; CLC Ministries International

About the Author:

Rayola Kelley, a seasoned minister of the Gospel, was born again and saved out of a cult in 1976 while serving in the U.S. Navy. Her spiritual journey continued through extensive discipleship, before following the Lord's call upon her life into full-time ministry in 1989, when, with Jeannette Haley, founded Gentle Shepherd Ministries.

Through the years, Rayola's gift of teaching the Word has opened many doors for her to teach adult Sunday school, oversee various fellowships for the last three decades, as well as hold evangelistic meetings in churches, conduct seminars, and speak at retreats. She has served in jail ministry, and is well known for her gift of spiritual insight and counseling.

Upon being called to be a missionary in America, Rayola, along with Jeannette Haley established different fellowships where intense Bible Studies and discipleship training were conducted to equip believers for the ministry. These different mission fields in America entailed working in various churches as well as working with other cultures such as Korean and Hispanic nationalities.

Rayola, along with co-laborer Jeannette Haley, (professional artist, author of Christian novels, Bible Studies and stories for children) began sending out a monthly newsletter containing articles for the Body of Christ in 1997 which continues to grow. Ms. Kelley has authored over 55 books, and numerous Bible Studies including an advanced Discipleship Course (available in both English and Spanish) that is being used in countries such as Africa, Bulgaria, Israel, Ireland, India, Cuba, and Pakistan.

Among her many books is *"Battle for the Soul"* which presents a clear picture of the battle that rages in the soul. She has written seven in-depth devotional books, including both the Old Testament and New Testament devotional study which takes the reader through the entire Bible in one year. All of her books are hard-hitting, bottom-line spiritual food for the hungry and thirsty soul to "chew" upon in order to *"grow strong in the Lord, and in the power of His might."*

Rayola currently resides in Oldtown, ID where she continues to fulfill Christ's commission to make disciples through teaching, spiritual counseling, and writing.

Please visit Gentle Shepherd Ministries Web Site at: www.gentleshepherd.com for further information, and to access her challenging and informative audio sermons.

Other books by Rayola Kelley:

Hidden Manna (Original)
Battle for the Soul (Book & Workbook)
Stories of the Heart
Transforming Love & Beyond
The Great Debate
Post to Post: (1) Establishing the Way
Post to Post: (2) Walking in the Way
Post to Post: (3) Meditations Along the Way

Volume One: Establishing Our Life in Christ

My Words are Spirit and Life
The Anatomy of Sin
The Principles of the Abundant Life
The Place of Covenant
Unmasking the Cult Mentality

Volume Two: Putting on the Life of Christ

He Actually Thought it Not Robbery
Revelation of the Cross
In Search of Real Faith
Think on These Things
Follow the Pattern

Volume Three: Developing a Godly Environment

Godly Discipline
Prayer and Worship
Don't Touch That Dial
Face of Thankfulness
ABC's of Christianity

Volume Four: Issues of the Heart

Hidden Manna (Revised)
Bring Down the Sacred Cows
The Manual for the Single Christian Life
Parents Are People Too

Volume Five: Challenging the Christian Life

The Issues of Life
Presentation of the Gospel
For the Purpose of Edification
Whatever Happened to the Church?
Women's Place in the Kingdom of God

Volume Six: Developing Our Christian Life

The Many Faces of Christianity
Possessing Our Souls
Experiencing the Christian Life
The Power of Our Testimonies
The Victorious Journey

Volume Seven: Discovering True Ministry
From Prisons and Dots to Christianity
So You Want To Be In Ministry?

Devotions
Devotions of the Heart: Books One and Two
Daily Food for the Soul: Books One and Two

Gentle Shepherd Ministries Devotion Series:
Being a Child of God
Disciplining the Strength of our Youth
Coming to Full Age

Nugget Books:
Nuggets From Heaven
More Nuggets From Heaven
Heavenly Gems
More Heavenly Gems
Heavenly Treasures

Gentle Shepherd Ministries Series:
The Christian Life Series
What Matter Is This?
The Challenge of It
The Reality of It
The Leadership Series
Overcoming
A Matter of Authority and Power
The Dynamics of True Leadership

Books By Jeannette Haley
Books co-authored with Rayola Kelley:
Hidden Manna (original)
The Many Faces of Christianity (Volume 6)
Post to Post 3: Meditations Along the Way

Other Books:
Rose of Light, Thorn of Darkness (Volume 7)
Interview in Hell (Volume 7)
Interview on Earth (Volume 7)
The Pig and I
Reflections of Wonder (Devotional)

Children's Books:
Little Stories for Little People
Traveler's Tales
The Adventures of Zack and Mira
The Adventures of Paul and Dana
(A House on the Beach)
The Monster of Mystery Valley